Please renew/return this item by the last date shown.

From Area codes 01923 or 020:	From Area codes of Herts:
Renewals: 01923 471373	01438 737373
Enquiries: 01923 471333	01438 737333
Textphone: 01923 471599	01438 737599

www.hertsdirect.org/librarycatalogue

hamlyn

A Pyramid Sport Paperback

Golf basics

Graham McColl

An Hachette Livre UK Company
www.hachettelivre.co.uk

A Pyramid Paperback

First published in Great Britain in 2005 by Hamlyn,
a division of Octopus Publishing Group Ltd
2–4 Heron Quays, London E14 4JP
www.octopusbooks.co.uk

This edition published in 2008

ISBN 978-0-600-61756-3

A CIP catalogue record for this book is available from the
British Library

Printed and bound in China

10 9 8 7 6 5 4 3 2 1

Publisher's note:
The text has been written from the point-of-view of
teaching a right-handed player. Reverse the advice
given for left-handed players to read 'left' for 'right'
and vice versa.

CONTENTS

The game of golf remains one of the few major sports that is not prejudiced against the fat person or thin, the tall or small, young or old. That is why it appeals to people from all walks of life.

Golf can be thrilling, exhilarating, frustrating and maddening. It can be any – or all – of these things to anyone. It is the game that launches a thousand questions.

- how long do you need to be playing to score respectably?

- how long before that complicated grip starts to feel comfortable?

- how do you stop slicing the ball?

This book attempts to answer some of the game's most pressing questions. Follow the tips and advice in these pages and you are sure to improve your game.

The average club golfer's handicap has remained virtually unchanged – at around 24 for men and 36 for ladies – for at least the past decade. The main reason for this is because very few golfers are committed and disciplined enough to go out and work on their game on a regular basis. If you do not spend enough time hitting balls on the range and practising your chipping and putting, you will never be able to turn the theory into reality.

The aim of this book is to provide you with all the information you need to put together a good, all-round game. You do not require a flawless technique in order to become a single-figure golfer. You simply have to become proficient in most areas of the game – particularly around the greens. And that is well within the reach of most club golfers.

EQUIPMENT

No game has been more affected by new technology than golf. Golf clubs and balls have been revolutionized in recent decades, and today's golfer is faced with an almost bewildering choice of equipment.

Clubs

Your first set of golf clubs will almost certainly have a textured, vulcanized rubber grip, perfect for use in all types of weather. However, many top players are now reverting to a version of the traditional leather grip, for greater feel, but that type of precise fine-tuning is only for the most advanced golfer.

As for the club shaft, the options are almost limitless. There is steel, boron, titanium or a pretty-coloured graphite from which to choose, and a wide range of flexes as well. Not surprisingly, many raw recruits emerge from their first visit to the local professional's shop or golfing superstore baffled and bewildered.

Although buying a set of golf clubs should feel special, it is best to treat the exercise in the same way as you would when making any other significant purchase. Decide how much you want to spend and remember that there's more than one type of club suitable for you.

If your budget is tight you can begin with a half-set of clubs – especially if you're a junior and not sure whether you are really going to like the game. Forget graphite, boron and the rest; a couple of metal-headed woods will be more than adequate to set you on your way. The majority of irons are cast-iron and cavity-backed. They are peripherally weighted, so that the weight is spread around the whole face of the club and not concentrated on the sweet spot, in the middle of the club. This means that shots played with such a modern, cavity-backed club are not as satisfying when they come out of the middle of the club as they are with the blade of a traditional-style iron, but they don't feel anywhere near as bad when the shot is mistimed. If you mis-hit with a blade, the ball will go nowhere, leaving you with a stinging sensation in your fingers. But the cast-iron club is much more forgiving, and is thus favoured by all but single-figure handicap golfers. A beginner shouldn't consider playing with anything else.

SECOND-HAND CLUBS

It is worth considering second-hand clubs. Avoid any set where the grooves in the face have become worn down through over-use. Also check the following:

- do the shafts show signs of rust, stress or wear and tear?

- are the grips in good condition? When you hold the club, the grips should live up to their name. Is the grip shiny? If so, it needs replacing.

Second-hand clubs represent a good investment if they are not too old. A good-quality set of second-hand clubs will serve you longer than a cheap set of new clubs.

Invest in your wedges

More than two-thirds of the shots you play during a round of golf will be struck from within 60 or 70 yards (55 or 64 metres) of the green – prime wedge territory. Most of the world's top golfers carry at least three wedges – a pitching wedge, a sand wedge and a lob wedge – in their bag (see pages 62–63). A few golfers, such as John Daly and Sweden's Jarmo Sandelin, actually carry four wedges to help them cope with the variety of different shots that they can face around the greens.

You do not need to go to that extreme but adding a lob wedge to your set is

It is worth investing in a putter you are comfortable with and that achieves results. Remember that you'll use this club more than any other in your bag.

advisable. Most amateur golfers will need to use a wedge regularly during the course of a round, but they will rarely use a 3-iron or a 2-iron. Consider leaving out one of the longer irons that you do not hit that often in favour of a specialist wedge. Your short game will improve dramatically.

Do not neglect or forget your putter

Many golfers are willing to spend a huge amount of money on a new driver, yet how many of those same golfers attach the same level of importance to purchasing a putter? Neglecting your putter when thinking about your set make-up is a very short-sighted attitude. You will use your putter almost twice as much during a round as your driver, so it makes sense to invest a little extra time and, possibly, money to find a model that you feel confident using and that complements your existing style of putting. Putting is all about feel.

As with the rest of the clubs in your set, putters come with a variety of different shaft lengths and lie angles, which means that, as with all your clubs, you should take the time to try some before you buy. A putter that boosts confidence when you hold it in your hands and look down at the ball is worth its weight in gold; so take your time choosing a make and model that you find inspirational. A good putter feels like a natural extension of the arms, giving pleasure each time you strike the ball.

Care and maintenance

Look after your clubs. Take a towel with you out on to the course and ensure that any mud or grass is cleaned from the face after any shot that has involved taking a divot. Always give the clubs a rinse and wipe down after each round. The last thing you want is dirt coming between the face of the club and the ball at impact. Always replace clubhead covers after every shot, not only to protect the faces of drivers or putters but also to prevent damage to club shafts. Especially if they are made of graphite.

Novice golfers needn't have too many long irons in their bag.

GOLF BALLS AND CLOTHING

Golf balls are made in a wide variety of performance styles with 1-, 2- or 3-piece cores, different cover materials and different dimple patterns. These affect the trajectory of the ball in flight, its behaviour off the clubface and what it does on landing. It is important to choose a ball that is suitable for the kind of clubs you use and for your style of play, especially your swing speed.

There are more than 1,000 legal golf balls from which you can choose the one that suits you best.

Balls

Although new technology has made a huge difference to golf clubs, the changes are nothing compared to developments in golf balls. In the late 19th century, balls couldn't fly more than 100 yards (91 metres) with a following wind; now they could travel five times that distance if the game's regulators at the Royal & Ancient Golf Club of St Andrews didn't impose strict controls. The improvements are vast even within the R&A's guidelines. In the 1970s, if you bought a dozen golf balls, two would, invariably, not be perfectly round, and a couple more would cut after a few blows. Now you will get 12 golf balls that conform exactly to the manufacturer's specifications.

The choice of balls is mind-boggling, so experiment with different kinds until you find a ball that you are comfortable using. Then stick to that type, because after playing with the same ball for an extended period of time you will improve your feel and get to know how that ball will react off the clubface with any given shot. This is important on and around greens, when judgement of pace is crucial. A recent survey found that even novices with inconsistent swings could feel the difference between a variety of types of ball. If you like the feel of a ball it will boost your confidence.

Ensure the golf shoes you buy fit as comfortably as possible. Remember you'll be walking more than 5 miles (8 km) each time you play.

Suitable clothing

Most private golf clubs have a dress code whereby denims and collarless shirts are usually forbidden. On municipal courses, however, there can be a sartorial free-for-all in which there is often not even any insistence on golf shoes being worn. You ought, though, to consider a rainsuit and proper golf shoes to be as essential to playing the game as a set of clubs. A bobble hat is always useful in bad weather, and a visor or a cap is equally welcome to wear on sunny days.

Golf shoes

Many players prefer golf shoes with metal spikes, which give better grip on wet or hilly ground. However, many golf clubs now insist that all players wear shoes fitted with soft spikes, made of rubber, to prevent damage to the greens.

It may seem an obvious point, but do make sure the shoes fit properly – there is absolutely nothing worse than reaching the farthest point on a golf course and then discovering that your new golf shoes are crippling you.

Rainwear

Rainsuits have improved immeasurably in recent years, with new lightweight fabrics that are designed not only to keep rain out but also to improve comfort while you swing the club without feeling inhibited. Before buying, try on any item that interests you to make sure that you can move freely. But be warned: rainsuits can be expensive.

MORE GOLFING ACCESSORIES

You can spend a small fortune on vast tour bags, heavy powered trolleys and gadgets and gizmos in profusion. But remember that in any competition you may not have more than 14 clubs in your bag (including your putter) and that gadgets to help you judge distance or line up your shot are all illegal.

Most bags come with automatic stands that ensure that both bag and clubs don't come into contact with wet grass.

Golf bags

Many regular golfers have two golf bags. One is designed to be placed on a trolley and will be of sturdy construction with ample pocket space to carry the necessary accessories. The other will be a lightweight bag for those days when the trolley cannot be used owing to wet conditions, or simply when the player fancies carrying his or her own clubs. When buying a golf bag:

- make sure the zips are of good quality and not likely to break or seize up;

- ensure there is a full hood that you can snap over the heads of the clubs when it is raining.

Tees, markers and other items

Most golf bags have plenty of room to carry items other than the clubs. In addition to golf balls, these accessories should include:

- wooden or plastic tees. As the name implies, for use only on the tee;

- a couple of ball markers to mark your ball on the green while you clean it before putting;

- a pitchmark repairer so you can repair any divots caused by the ball thudding into the green;

- a couple of towels: one to keep the grips dry in inclement weather; the other, which you can attach to your bag for ease of access, to clean your ball before putting and before driving off;

- a couple of pencils for filling in your scorecard;

- a golf umbrella.

Trolleys

Among optional items is a golf trolley to hold your golf bag. For many golfers, trolleys are an essential item since they take the strain out of carrying a full bag. Equally, many golfers can't stand the sight of them. They don't feel that they're playing proper golf unless the bag is slung over the shoulder. Most trolleys are lightweight and easily collapsible for practical storage.

Golf trolleys have also been greatly helped by new technology. Some are now so computerized that, at the press of a button, they will propel themselves down a fairway, leaving the player encumbered with nothing more than a small remote-control gadget to carry.

Golfing gloves

A glove is another accessory that is an essential item for some golfers and optional for others. There are some top professionals, such as Fred Couples, who cannot see any use for a glove at all.

Most players, however, use one as it helps to keep a firm grip on the club. Remember,

A glove will prevent the grip from slipping in your hands.

if you're a right-handed golfer you need a left-handed glove, since it is the left hand that grips the club. The glove should fit snugly: not so tightly that the leather stitching is strained, but not so loosely that there's a spare ½ inch (1 cm) at the end of each finger.

Protecting your clubs

Headcovers today serve two purposes: they protect the soft faces of putters and some types of metal woods; they also protect the shafts of those clubs made of graphite or other complex materials. To avoid damage always replace headcovers before putting a club back in the bag.

THE GRIP

The grip is the foundation of a good swing, and a good golfer who has a bad grip will find that his or her game suffers severely. The grip is the only contact a player has with the golf club, so great care must be taken with it.

Bad habits, especially those concerning the fundamentals of the swing, are difficult to shake off, so you should aim to make holding the club correctly an instinctive part of your game. The grip will determine a player's wrist position, the plane of their swing and the amount of power they can generate.

Getting a grip

Top players are very careful about the way they form their grip, and amateur golfers must be no less disciplined. A good grip should be as natural as possible. If you stand up and let your arms hang naturally by your sides, the palms and forearms turn inward slightly towards the thighs. This is how your hands should look when holding the golf club. When the hands are moulded together like this, the player has the best chance of hitting a powerful, accurate shot.

The illustrated guidelines that follow are written for a right-handed player; switch left for right and vice versa if they are to be applied to a left-handed player.

If you watch a professional practising before a tournament he or she almost invariably has a coach looking on to check that all parts of their game are working correctly. You will often see them checking the grip because even though a minor change in the grip may be imperceptible to the player, it can have a considerable effect on the way the club strikes the ball. It is worth having a good teaching professional check your grip and set-up from time to time. It is amazing how these things can gradually deteriorate.

CORRECT GRIP

There are several ways that a player can link their hands together on the club. Tiger Woods and Jack Nicklaus favour the interlocking grip, but most other top players use the Vardon (or overlapping) grip, and many coaches recommend that juniors start off using the baseball grip. The decision is really one of personal choice, so try out all the main types of grip before settling on the method that you find most comfortable.

Three steps to a correct grip

1 Allow the grip of the club to run along the base of the fingers on your left hand. The index finger is used to form a slight 'trigger'.

2 When you have closed your left hand round the club your left thumb should be pointing straight down at the ground, slightly to the right of centre on the grip. You should be able to see two or three knuckles of the left hand. As you position your right hand on the club, the grip of the club is again at the base of tho fingors.

3 The grip is completed when you close your right hand on the club, so that the lifeline of the right palm rests on top of the left thumb, covering it completely. If the grip is made correctly, you should be able to see two knuckles on the right hand.

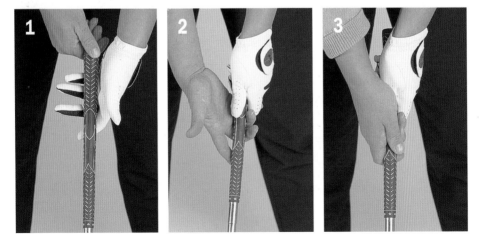

GRIP OPTIONS

Neutral grip

A neutral grip, where neither left nor right hand dominates, gives the player the best possible chance of returning the clubface squarely to the target line at the point of impact.

Strong grip

If you can see more than three knuckles on the left hand and fewer than two on your right, the grip is too strong. You will be likely to hook or top many shots.

Weak grip

If you can see fewer than two knuckles on the left hand and more than two on your right, the grip is too weak. You will be likely to slice or block shots out to the right.

Interlocking grip

The interlocking grip is favoured by golfers with small hands. It is similar to the Vardon grip (see right), but the little finger on the right hand and the left index finger interlock rather than overlap.

Vardon grip

Named after the famous British golfer Harry Vardon, this grip is often referred to as the overlap grip, as the little finger on the right hand rests in the groove between the index and second finger on the left hand. This is the most popular grip among low-handicappers.

Baseball grip

Juniors are often encouraged to use the baseball grip. The hands are placed side by side on the grip, without any link, so there's more freedom of movement, making it easier to 'break' the wrists and release the club.

THE SWING

Ask any top golfer to offer one piece of advice and invariably they will say that the key to good golfing is to work on the fundamentals of the game right from the outset. The grip, posture and clubface alignment are easily overlooked but they are undoubtedly the most important aspects of the game on which to focus, and if you get them right all else should flow from there.

If you do not hold the club properly, nor aim carefully and address the ball correctly, your swing will be a shambles, and if your swing is a shambles your golf won't be enjoyable. At worst, you will struggle to make good contact on the ball. At best, your swing will be riddled with compensations to counteract your sloppy basics, all of which will eat away at your power and accuracy.

The world's top golfers are meticulous about the way in which they hold the club, address the ball, aim the clubface and shape their body. They know that if they encounter a swing problem on the course, most of the time it can be traced back to an anomaly at address. The moral of the story is that you will maximize your chances of having a good swing if you eradicate errors at the set-up stage (see pages 22–23).

Correct alignment

If the grip is the most badly abused of all the swing fundamentals, then alignment is probably the most neglected – by players of all levels. To hit consistently straight shots, the clubface must not only be aimed at your target correctly but also be aligned squarely to your body. If the clubface and your feet, hips and shoulders are at odds with each other, you will struggle to swing the club on the correct path, making it difficult to strike the ball powerfully and accurately.

It is worth taking a few lessons with a good teaching professional so that you are able to align the clubface and your body correctly. You will then have a clear understanding of what you are trying to achieve and how to achieve it consistently on the course.

SHOULDER ALIGNMENT

After aiming the clubface carefully, the next key area of the alignment process is the positioning of your shoulders. Many amateurs concentrate more on where the feet are aiming, but you do not hit the ball with the feet. It is the position of the shoulders that dictates the line of the swing path, so it is vital that the upper body is aligned correctly. The feet should be placed square to the target.

On the practice ground

The majority of the world's top players constantly monitor their alignment because it is very difficult to see where the clubface and the body are aiming when you are standing right on top of the ball. For this very reason, you will often notice the professionals lay a club on the ground parallel to their target line as a reference point for their alignment routine. This enables them to aim the clubface and position their feet and shoulders correctly, prior to every single practice shot they hit. It also serves to condition the feelings associated with the correct alignment position so that there is less chance that things will go wrong when it comes to hitting shots on the golf course itself.

Aim body and clubface

Golfers of all levels struggle with their alignment for the simple reason that, when the ball is hit, they are standing side on to a target that is up to 200 yards (183 metres) away. Poor alignment is a very common set-up flaw. Many golfers make the mistake of setting up over the ball before even thinking about aiming their body and the clubface. However, such an approach is a recipe for disaster.

Practise with a club laid out on the ground to get your alignment routine correct.

Address routine

Good alignment takes its lead from the position of the clubface:

- make sure that you start your address routine by carefully aiming the clubface at your intended target;

- once you have done that, you then have a reference point from which you can aim your body – feet, hips and shoulders – squarely to that initial line;

- keep checking your alignment as you position your body and feet.

A good way to hone this routine on the driving range is to place two clubs on the ground parallel to each other as guides. After hitting several shots with the clubs in place you will soon develop an instinctive awareness for the correct target line, and this will prove invaluable when out on the course for real.

On the course use marks on the ground, patches of darker grass, loose twigs or other features on the line between ball and target to check alignment.

Check and double-check

1 Aim the clubface at your intended target. Do not let the club move off line as you move your feet and body.

2 Constantly refer to the target as you aim the clubface and position your upper body. Check and double-check that the clubface is aiming where you want the ball to go.

3 Position your feet. Visualize the shot you are about to make and check, again, that the clubface is aiming at the target.

USING A PRE-SHOT ROUTINE

If you watch the world's top golfers in action, you will notice that, without exception, each has a routine that is unerringly followed before each shot. Whether hitting a driver off the first tee or a simple approach shot with a pitching wedge, the top stars never alter their routine.

Seeking consistency

There are two main reasons why the world's top players are so precise about their pre-shot routines:

- they know that the quality of their shots is largely determined by the quality of their basics (that is, the way in which they grip the club and address the ball). By incorporating these fundamentals into a routine, the top players maximize their chances of settling into the correct address position;

- human beings are creatures of habit. We perform tasks more effectively after repeated rehearsal. If a routine is ingrained enough, it will automatically

be followed as soon as the club is taken out of the bag. And if the first part of the routine is the same every time, the last part – in this case the golf swing itself – will also be the same.

Take Nick Faldo, for example. If you time his routine from the moment he picks up his club until he starts his backswing, you will find that it varies by no more than a fraction of a second for each shot he plays. If Faldo is disturbed while going through his routine, he will start again from the beginning, even going so far as putting the club back in the bag and taking it out again.

A player's pre-shot routine is unique to them and is full of idiosyncrasies. There are, however, several components that all players should be encouraged to incorporate into their own routines (see opposite). By standing behind the ball, looking towards the target, it is easy to identify a mark on the ground a few feet in front of the ball on the line to the target. It is then possible to keep that mark in view at the address position, which makes checking alignment much easier. In addition, visualizing the shot is much easier when standing behind the ball, and you should visualize every shot you play, even on the practice ground.

Pre-shot routine

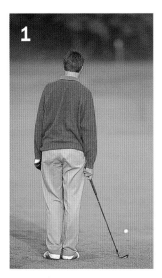

1 Once you have assessed the shot and are comfortable with your club selection and strategy, you should stand directly behind the ball to the target line and visualize the shot you are about to play.

2 A right-handed player should then approach the ball from the left, stepping into the shot with the right foot and setting the clubface behind the ball, while the right hand aligns itself square to the intended line of flight.

3 Complete your stance by bringing the left foot forward, ensuring as you do so that your feet aim parallel to, but left of, the target.

4 Once you have applied your left hand to the grip, check your aim, giving the club a quick waggle to relieve the tension in the forearms. Only then should you set your swing in motion.

SWINGING INTO ACTION

Once you have developed a sound understanding of the basic fundamentals, you can develop your swing so that it is technically proficient and consistent, reliable and powerful in the upper body coil. The coiling motion of the upper body is the core of any good golf swing. If the upper body rotates correctly around your spine angle then you have a very good chance of creating power and striking the ball cleanly. Your arms create width, power and leverage in the swing, yet many amateur golfers fail to make full use of this key power source. As your upper body coils and turns back and through, your arms swing up and down.

Wrist hinge

Together with the swinging motion of your arms, the wrists are another source of power that many golfers fail to utilize correctly. Good wrist action plays an important role in enabling the club to find the correct plane in the backswing so that it can approach the ball on the correct angle and path.

The lower body

Your lower body – legs, hips and feet – are the support of your swing as well as a key source of power in their own right. If your lower body gives way during the backswing, you will be unable to coil your shoulders correctly and create maximum power.

Fluent movements

Once you have developed all of the key areas of the golf swing, the next step is to blend those individual elements together into one free-flowing motion. No matter how technically accomplished you are, unless your swing has a good rhythm and tempo, it will simply be a series of disjointed motions. Above all, a good golf swing is a function of good balance.

One of the best ways to learn about the golf swing is to study the techniques of the world's top players. Sweden's Per-Ulrik Johansson has one of the most efficient swings in the world of professional golf. Most players could learn much from his method (see pages 27, 28 and 29).

Johansson's golf stance

1 At address, Johansson adopts an athletic posture, with his body aligned squarely to the target. The body angles created here will be maintained throughout the entire swing.

2 At the top of the swing, his hands are above his right shoulder, with the club shaft square to the target line. The spine angle remains as it was at address and the knees are still bent.

3 At impact, Johansson's hips are open to the target, while his shoulders are in virtually a square position.

4 Even in the follow-through position, you can still see the angles Johansson created at address.

Johansson's swing from the front

1 With an iron, Johansson's hands are slightly ahead of the ball with their weight evenly balanced; his feet are about shoulder-width apart.

2 The clubhead stays low to the ground for the first couple of feet (0.5 metres) of the swing. At this point, Johansson's shoulders begin to turn in response to the swinging motion created by his arms.

4 A good downswing starts from the ground upward. From the top of the swing, Johansson nudges his left knee towards the target and begins to clear his hips out of the way. He will also retain his wrist angle for as long as possible into the downswing.

5 The moment of truth. At the point of impact, the shaft of the club and the left arm should form as straight a line as possible in order to apply maximum pressure to the ball. Most of Johansson's weight is now on his left side.

3 By the time they reach the top of their backswing, Johansson's wrists will have fully 'broken' and his shoulders will have turned 90 degrees. See how both his knees remain bent and how the right knee in particular has resisted the turning of the upper body.

6 A good follow-through is the product of a good swing. Johansson's weight will be on his front foot and his chest will be facing the target. All the spikes on his back foot should now be visible.

Downswing checklist

- Transfer weight on to your left side as you start down
- Start downswing with your left hip
- Don't start with your right shoulder or arms
- Hold your wrist hinge on way down
- At point of impact, hips are open to target, weight is on left and left knee is straight
- Release powerfully through impact and extending arms
- Make a full balanced finish

Impact checklist

- Head behind ball
- Wrists straightened at impact
- Weight on left side
- Left knee moves forward over front foot

THE FOLLOW-THROUGH

The follow-through is when you uncoil and realize all your potential. That's the theory, anyway. Having got the backswing right, don't spoil it all by coming down from the top like a hurricane entering Miami Beach. Keep that right arm nicely straight. Maintain your rhythm. Keep your eye on the ball. Let it all unfold naturally. It all sounds so easy doesn't it?

end, with your right toe pointing towards the ground. Grasp all that and the ball will travel 200 yards (183 metres). Be prepared for a few hiccups along the way and just remember:

- never get so discouraged that you feel like giving up;

- never get so encouraged that you think you're perfect.

Developing your own swing
Some of the great golfers had swings that made an orthodox player weep and that

Balance
Make sure your body turns throughout and doesn't tilt. This is one of the most common faults in golf. It is caused because the player is so anxious to give the ball a helping hand that they lean back as they begin their follow-through. The result is disastrous. Just practise that turning sensation in your living room. Feel your upper body turning to the right during the backswing and then back towards the centre during the first part of the follow-through, then your whole body turning towards the left during the second part. You should be perfectly balanced at the

defied supposedly golden rules. Gary Player couldn't swing the club without knocking himself over – so much for perfect balance. Arnold Palmer attacked the ball as if it was threatening his life – so much for smooth rhythm. In his prime, Jack Nicklaus committed a cardinal sin – his right elbow refused to remain tucked against his side at the top of the backswing. The achievements of these three, who ruled over golf's record books for 40 years until Tiger Woods came along, should convince you there is room for an individualistic swing.

The message, therefore, is clear; if something is working for you, don't go and change it – just go out and enjoy your golf and to hell with worrying whether it looks right or not. It is important to grasp, though, that there are fundamentals that, if implemented in your swing, will make you a more consistent golfer. Jim Furyk's idiosyncratic swing was good enough under pressure to help him claim the 2003 US Open Championship.

There's no better feeling than when all of the elements of the swing come together in a natural, flowing movement that enables you to hit the ball straight and far.

THE LONG GAME

Professional golfers think that the long game is all a bit of an exercise in puffing out the chest and showing off a little. How else would the saying, 'Drive for show, putt for dough' have come into being? In a way they're right. A good drive more than any other aspect of golf emphasizes the difference between the average player and the golfer they aspire to become.

Accuracy before distance

For the newcomer to the game or the moderate golfer who wishes to improve, the long game should not in any way be about showing off. You should aim simply to improve your driving technique so that you can regularly hit the fairway and carry the ball around 200 yards (183 metres) off the tee. You should also try to improve your long game so that you can hit your approach shots on to the green around 50 per cent of the time.

Although a competent short game can often compensate for errant driving and approach play, improving your long game is without doubt the quickest way to improve your handicap. If you can carry the ball a reasonable distance off the tee with a good level of accuracy, the rest of the hole becomes easier because your next shot is played with a shorter and more controllable club. That inevitably means that you have a better chance of hitting the ball on to the green and closer to the hole. Improving the quality of your long game will thus have a knock-on effect on the rest of your game, inevitably leading to lower scores.

Male golfers

If you're a man, part of your long-game problem may not be about technique at all but about keeping your macho tendencies in check. The next time you watch Tiger Woods or Ernie Els, don't admire the flight of the ball and how far it travels, but study the things from which you can learn. For example, how they concentrate; the rhythm of their action; and the variety of clubs that they use to cope with the differing demands of each hole. So forget fear and step on to the tee with a spring in your stride and confidence in your heart.

LONG-RANGE SHOTS

Fairway woods and long irons are invariably troublesome to the average golfer and it is important to know what you should do when you're in a divot and how you should cope with such quandaries as being stuck with a downhill or sloping lie. This section will teach you how to play each long-range shot with the minimum of effort.

Clubs and distance

These days, 'woods' are not made from wood at all. They're invariably composed of metal and they make a ghastly sound when they meet the back of the ball. There are consolations: the ball goes farther; and the new generation of metal woods is very forgiving so even a badly mis-hit shot will travel a fair distance.

With both irons and woods the number of the club indicates its potential with regard to how far the ball will travel. The lower the wood number, the less degree of loft on the clubface, the longer the shaft, and so the farther you can hit the ball. The driver or 1-wood, therefore, is the most powerful club in a golfer's armoury. It is usually used to hit tee shots on par 4s and par 5s, and is the club that hits the ball farthest. Phil Mickelson regularly propels the ball 350 yards (320 metres) with his driver. An average player will hit it about 220 yards (200 metres), although many amateurs find it one of the most difficult clubs to use.

It is the straight face on a driver that causes the problems. A typical driver will possess a loft angle of just ten degrees. Many are intimidated by it, believing that they will never get the ball airborne, so they try to help the process along, usually with fatal consequences. (For the correct driver technique see pages 36–37.) Best, then, to start with a 2- or 3-wood, which is more helpful to the beginner. The former is basically a substitute driver and so really only suitable for use off a tee.

Three-wood

The 3-wood is a much more versatile club than the 2-wood, and its 15-degree loft allows a player to use it if the ball is lying in a good position on the fairway. This club is the one with which you really do need to make friends. Most players find that they have far greater accuracy with it than the driver and the loss of 15–20 yards (14–18 metres) is, for the most part, inconsequential if you're on the fairway eight times out of ten instead of just two or three. Armed with this sort of philosophy, the Australian Peter Thomson once won the Open at Royal Birkdale without ever taking the driver out of his bag.

Four-wood and beyond

The 4-wood is an even more friendly piece of equipment but its 18-degree loft means you start to lose distance. It is ideal, though, for tee shots to narrow fairways, or fairway blows where the lie is none too favourable. You will even be able to use it in some instances in the rough.

Many players, even some pros, have realized that modern 5-, 7- and 9-woods are easier to hit from a variety of lies than their equivalent iron clubs. For the less athletic player, the sweeping stroke used to hit these clubs is easier and more comfortable for them than the powerful, crisp striking needed for the longer irons.

There are also new generations of rescue clubs, a sort of hybrid between irons and woods which cover all sorts of shot-making, from long fairway shots to clipping.

Modern metal woods are much easier to hit for the average player than old persimmon woods.

Cavity-back irons (left) are more forgiving for most players. Low handicappers and professionals often prefer the extra feel of blades (right), but they must be hit very precisely.

DRIVING – SWEEPING THE BALL AWAY

The driver is the least forgiving club in the bag, so it is vital that your set-up and swing are as accurate as possible. Players may get away with small flaws in their swing when playing with shorter irons, but with the driver any faults are ruthlessly exposed.

Driver set-up

The priority for shots played with the driver is to create clubhead speed. The aim should be to sweep the ball off the tee and into the air with a shallow angle of attack. To make this easier, the player's weight should favour their right side at address and the ball should be played well forward in the stance, just inside the left heel. The player's hands should be even with, or fractionally behind, the ball at address. The swing should start with the clubhead low to the ground to set

Points to remember when using a driver

1 Because of the lack of loft on the face of a driver, you need to place the ball on a tee peg and play it forward in your stance to get it airborne.

2 Focus on keeping your swing as smooth and controlled as possible throughout.

up a wide takeaway. The driver is the longest club in the bag, so it is important to give yourself plenty of room and to control its power. To do this you must retain the bend in the right knee and prevent your weight from moving on to the outside of the right foot. To maximize power, you must make the transition between backswing and downswing as smooth as possible. Any sudden lunges will destroy rhythm and almost certainly lead to a loss of power and distance.

At impact, the left arm and club should form a straight line because the clubface makes contact with the ball slightly on the upswing while the clubhead is released past the body. At the finishing position, your weight should be supported by the left leg and right toe and your chest should be facing the target.

3 At the top of the backswing, the shaft of your driver should be horizontal to the ground and aiming squarely to your intended target.

4 It is vital that you stay behind the ball through impact so that the clubface can sweep the ball off the tee with a shallow angle of attack. Keep your head behind the ball. Don't lunge with your shoulders.

5 The length of the driver and the momentum of your swing will pull you round into a full finish position. Always finish with your weight on your front foot and your right shoulder nearest the target.

FROM THE TEE

As the purpose of the driver is to sweep the ball away off the top of the tee, a small but important point for all players to consider is the height at which to tee up the ball. Ideally, you should be able to see the top half of the ball above the top of the clubhead at the address position.

Tee the ball so that half of it is above your clubhead.

Before you address the ball

Practise poise and concentration before taking your tee shot. We've all been guilty of chatting away from the moment we leave one green to the moment we tee up the ball on the next hole, then swishing away at the ball only to see it finish in trouble. There's an easy way to avoid this. Just give yourself a moment as you step on to the tee to work out exactly what you are trying to do. You don't have to be slow about it but making a mental picture of what you want to achieve is vital to success. After you've hit the ball, you can chat away again to your heart's content.

Assess your shot

Before you play your tee shot, take a moment to weigh up the hole's character. Visualize the shot you want to play and what you hope to leave yourself with for your second stroke. It is not always necessary or appropriate to use the driver to hit your tee shot. If a long drive will leave you with a wedge to the green and you are currently not speaking to your wedge, then take a 3-wood instead and leave yourself an 8-iron.

Aiming accurately

Once you've decided on the shot you want to make and the correct line, find something on the green or the skyline at which to aim and set yourself up accordingly. It may even be the flag itself, but it is crucial to have something on which to focus. Setting an intermediate target will help you deal with any intimidating factors such as deep fairway bunkers or trees on either side. Block out these features and concentrate on the object at which you have decided to aim.

You should seek tiny targets for better accuracy. Pick out a really small target in the distance. It can be a branch of a tree, a chimney on a house, anything on which you can focus. By aiming at a small area, you will narrow your margin for error and give your brain a clear instruction. The wider your target, the wider the scope for inaccuracy.

To help with lining up, Jack Nicklaus – one of the greatest drivers of all time – would look at the ball, then at a spot 18 inches (45 cm) in front of it, then at the place down the fairway where he hoped his ball would finish. He would draw an imaginary line along all three. If he felt the line was at all crooked, he would adjust accordingly. It's got to be worth a try if it was good enough for the greatest golfer of all.

A good posture and set-up have allowed this golfer to concentrate entirely on the target and his alignment.

CLUB SELECTION

It's a failing of many players that during a round they will use only one club off the tee for the 14 or so holes that are par fours or fives. For example, they erroneously reach for a driver when confronted with a hole of 500 yards (460 metres) with two deep bunkers that narrow the fairway to just 20 yards (18 metres) in width at about the distance to which they can hit. On a hole of 320 yards (292 metres) with a narrow sliver of fairway at which to aim, owing to water down the left-hand side and trees on the right, they pull out the driver ... and so on.

Careful planning

It is interesting to note that the straightest drivers of all, such as Colin Montgomerie or Lee Westwood, wouldn't dream of using a driver in either of these instances unless there were three holes to play and they needed three birdies. Even given that situation, they would probably still use other clubs.

Many golfers fall back on the argument that they are just having a fun round and using a 3-wood on one hole and a 3-iron on another would go against the grain. That is fine, of course, but on the really fun rounds that you have enjoyed you can be sure that you were playing well and scoring well. Most golfers would answer in the affirmative to both these questions. Yet taking a driver on every hole helps them achieve neither; indeed, driving into the water or into the trees can have just the opposite effect, as your score goes haywire and your confidence disappears down the drain.

So if the fairway is narrow at the driving distance, don't look on it as an irresistible temptation, but concede a small defeat to the course and use your 3-wood in the knowledge that you'll have a much better chance of winning a far greater victory by enjoying success on the hole. Or use your 4-wood if you think the situation calls for it.

Know the yardages of every club in your bag

Knowing what you can comfortably achieve with each club you have is the first step to improving your course management. It's this vital information that will determine your strategy on every shot. Without that knowledge at your disposal, your club selection on any shot is nothing more than guesswork.

Ensure you spend plenty of time on the driving range assessing your range with each club. Do not let your ego get in the way of recording your accurate yardage. Most amateur golfers claim that they can hit their 7-iron 150 yards (137 metres), but when you consider that Nick Price hits his only 155 yards (142 metres), it is highly unlikely that the average club golfer is just 5 yards (5 metres) behind. In fact, most amateurs are closer to 130 yards (119 metres) with their 7-iron.

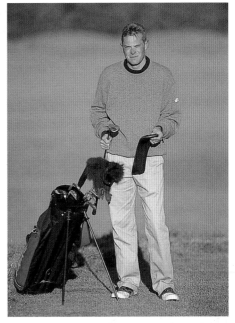

Think carefully before selecting the wood you use from the tee.

THE YARDAGE TEST

Take ten balls on to the practice field. After hitting all ten balls, walk up the range – ideally with a yardage wheel. Ignoring your two best and worst shots, measure the remaining six balls and take an average of the combined total. Like it or not, that is your yardage with that club. Repeat the process with every club in the bag and complete this table. It will be one of your most productive practice sessions ever.

Club	Yardage	Club	Yardage
Sand wedge		4-iron	
Pitching wedge		3-iron	
9-iron		2-iron	
8-iron		1-iron	
7-iron		4-wood	
6-iron		3-wood	
5-iron		1-wood	

USING LONG IRONS

If there are two words that are guaranteed to induce a long face from the average player, they must be 'long irons'. There's no disguising the fact that the 1- and 2-irons are the hardest clubs in the bag to use. The loft on a 1-iron is slightly less than that on a 3-wood, and a 2-iron is the equivalent of a 4-wood, but the margin for error with an iron is much greater than with a wood. Those 2-irons are strictly for low-handicap amateurs and professionals. But come down to the 3- or 4-irons, with their greater loft, and here we have clubs that can be used by most players.

Practice is the name of the game here. You need to spend some time just hitting 3- and 4-irons to develop the confidence to use them when you go out on to the golf course. The 5- and 6-irons, meanwhile, should be among the most accurate clubs in your bag.

Finding the club you're comfortable with

It is terribly important to know how far you hit your long irons, so make sure you've completed the table on page 41 and feel confident in the club you are using. There's nothing more frustrating than hitting a gorgeous 3-iron to a difficult long par three and seeing it pitch 20 yards (18 metres) over the pin and into trouble at the back of the green.

From the tee

Another instance that shows up the difference between the way professional and amateur golfers think is in the use of

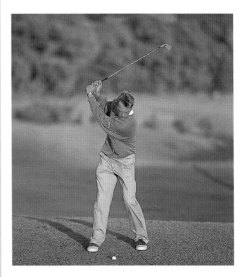

Confidence in your long irons will come only through practice.

A DILEMMA OF CLUB CHOICE

Here's a little scenario: the first par three you play is 170 yards (155 metres) and you strike a 4-iron beautifully into the heart of the green. The second par three is 190 yards (174 metres), downwind, and so you take another 4-iron and again you strike it well. The next hole is a short par four and the trouble is such that it requires another tee shot of 170 yards (155 metres). What should you do now? What most professionals would do is take out a 4-iron. However, even when the logic of taking this iron is staring them in the face, most amateurs would still prefer to hit a 'soft' fairway wood.

The problem is clearly a mental one. You've hit two perfectly acceptable 4-iron shots to short holes. Why not use the same club when there is a much bigger target to find, namely the broader expanse of the fairway? Conquering the mental barrier of using an iron in these circumstances and finding one in which you have confidence – be it a 2-, 3- or 4-iron – is one of the keys to scoring well. There may be nothing like hitting a wood as straight as an arrow, but equally there's nothing more sure to wreck a scorecard than gambling with a driver and losing. Going for glory all too often results in embarrassment and disaster.

an iron off the tee. Most pros consider it an essential part of their armoury to have a long iron that they can reliably use off the tee to find the fairway. Most amateurs use one off the tee only when it is required on a short hole.

The nervy tee shot

It's perhaps even more important to find a long iron you're happy with from the tee, particularly if you are a novice golfer and aren't consistent with your driving. The first tee can be particularly scary with other playing partners and golfers (even sometimes the whole of the clubhouse bar!) watching you. So take a 4- or 5-iron that you know you can hit comfortably and smoothly; then place yourself on the fairway – away from the galleries.

Using an iron from the tee provides pleasing levels of accuracy.

FAIRWAY WOOD OR IRON?

So you're in the middle of the fairway, you've got a smashing lie, and the green is 200 yards (183 metres) away. What do you do now? What you don't do is what eight out of ten amateurs do: dash back to the bag and wrench the cover off the 3-wood as fast as you can. A glory shot may be a tempting option but if you have a water hazard on the left and a bunker on the right, you can end up in a whole lot of trouble. The only shot you may be able to visualize is one that flies straight and true, leaving you just 20 feet (6 metres) from the hole and set up nicely for a birdie three. But before you attempt to conjure up reality from fantasy, it is best to step back and think.

Before you take out that 3-wood, answer this question:

"How many times do you complete that perfect stroke, particularly when inhibiting factors are present and the green is so well protected?"

Comfortably avoiding hazards

Most players are delighted if they hit the perfect shot once in 20 occasions. On the other 19 they will either lose their ball in the lake or find themselves confronted by a nasty sand shot. Here is a far better strategy when confronted by hazards on either side of a green that seems easily within reach. Take an iron or a smaller wood, so as to leave yourself a shot of 20 yards (18 metres) to the green. That way, you take out of play both the lake and the bunker. Admittedly, you won't get a birdie three. But you will get a four or, perhaps at worst, a bogey five, which is certainly better than the score you would be looking at if you were staring forlornly at your ball in the water.

When to use the wood

There are times when a 3- or 4-wood is a perfectly good option. If, for example, you are three holes down with four to play and your opponent is already on the putting surface in two, then clearly you have no choice. Dire circumstances call for drastic measures. Maybe the entrance to the green is wide open, or you think you could give Ernie Els a game out of the sand. In those circumstances, by all means go ahead and blaze away.

Much depends on how the ball is lying. Lush grass may give a nice lie, giving you the confidence to strike boldly, but from a tight, bare lie caution is prudent. The key is to let the stars clear from your eyes and then assess the shot in a calculating manner. If the penalties for straying off-line around the green are great, then go with an iron. Don't risk leaving yourself a shot you dread. Above all, don't throw careless shots away when a little bit of caution can make things easier for you.

A fairway wood is one of the most effective weapons in the golf bag.

SLOPING LIES

The major problem that slopes present is that they move the ball from its normal position in the stance – either further forward or back, or higher or lower – leaving most golfers unsure of what to do next. Given the option of adjusting their address position or improvizing their swing to reach the ball, most players wrongly take the latter option.

Addressing the ball

The key to playing from any kind of slope – uphill, downhill or sidehill – is to set up in such a way that you can still use your normal swing to play the shot (see pages 26–31). It is better to adjust your address position (see page 23) than to manufacture a swing that you have never tried before. When the ball is above your feet, for example, you should stand a little more upright and choke down on the grip to compensate for the fact that the ball is nearer your body. When the ball is below your feet, the opposite approach should be taken.

Uphill lie

On an uphill lie, you have a ready-made launch pad to help get the ball airborne, so remember to allow for the higher ball flight by taking a less-lofted club to achieve a similar distance as you would from a flat lie. To bring your shoulders in line with the slope, place a little extra weight on your right leg at address and keep your right shoulder low. This will allow you to swing along and up the slope through impact, rather than straight into it.

Downhill lie

When the ball is on a downslope, the gradient removes loft from the clubface, thereby causing the ball to follow a lower trajectory. Allow for this by selecting a slightly more lofted club to play the shot. In this case, when you bring your shoulders in line with the slope you automatically set a little extra weight on your left side. Your left shoulder should feel lower than the right at address. From this address position, the steeper takeaway will enable you to clear the slope.

On uphill and downhill lies, the first thing to do is to amend your set-up so that your shoulders are as close as possible to level with the slope in question. By doing this, you effectively recreate a flat lie, which enables you to use your normal swing to play the shot.

Slow and smooth

Your final consideration when playing from any kind of slope is that you should swing as smoothly as possible. Any time you are confronted with a shot that is slightly out of the norm, the temptation is to swing too quickly to get it over and done with, and the end result is usually less than impressive, leading to an even greater lack of confidence the next time. A smooth tempo will often compensate for technical flaws in your swing, so even if you are unsure about how to amend your address position, if you can remain calm enough to swing smoothly you will have a good chance of playing the shot.

Ball above feet

When the ball is above the level of your feet, you should stand more upright at address and choke down on the grip of the club. Your more upright spine angle will produce a flatter and more rounded swing path, which will cause the ball to curve from right to left in the air. You can compensate for this by aiming right of your intended target.

Ball below feet

When the ball is below your feet, it is farther away from you. Allow for this by tilting forwards more with your body, increasing your knee flex and gripping the club towards the end of the handle. The tendency is to swing the club on a steep plane, which produces a shot that flies from left to right. Allow for this by aiming left of your intended target.

PLAYING OUT OF THE ROUGH

You should never underestimate the resistance that grass will put up against your swing when playing a shot out of thick and heavy rough. Even light, fluffy fringe grass – or semi rough – that you often find lurking inconspicuously just off the edge of the fairway is enough to get between the ball and the clubface, taking a considerable number of yards (metres) off your shot.

Play it rough

There are two things you should remember when faced with this situation:

- when hitting out of the rough, you must accept that there is no substitute for strength. There are certain techniques that you can use to make the shot easier but ultimately power plays a key role in removing your ball from the rough. You have to swing hard. Unfortunately, there is no other option available;

- you should try to create a steeper attack into the ball in the downswing so that you avoid swinging the clubhead through

lots of thick and heavy grass in front of the ball that will inevitably slow your swing speed down considerably. With this in mind, you will find it helpful to set up with a little extra weight on your left side; this will make it easier for you to hit down on the ball through impact. Most top players will also open the clubface at address because they know that the grass is likely to wrap itself around the clubhead through impact, closing the face and producing a low shot that travels sharply to the left, usually into even deeper trouble.

Assess your chances

Weigh up the risks involved when playing out of the rough and think realistically. Many amateur golfers underestimate how much the thick rough will affect their shot, and they still believe that they can hit the ball almost as far as they can from the fairway. Unfortunately, that is not the case. Check your ego before attempting to blast the ball out of heavy grass. Unless your ball is lying perfectly and sitting up nicely in thick rough, do not even think about playing anything other than one of your wedges or a mid-iron at most: anything else is just not worth the risk. Nine times out of ten the sensible strategy is to get the ball safely back on to the fairway.

Show commitment

Once you have amended your address position (see page 23), pick the club up fairly steeply in your backswing and then concentrate on hitting purposefully down and through. One hundred per cent commitment is essential, since anything less than a full swing will make it difficult for you to achieve any great distance.

If the ball is lying in deep, thick rough you have little option other than to use a wedge simply to get the ball back in play on the fairway. However, from semi-rough a 4- or 5-wood may be a better choice, for its broad, flat sole will ride the grass rather than digging into it as an iron might do.

Making a clean escape from deep, thick rough

1 To avoid swinging the clubhead through lots of thick grass in front of the ball, play the ball back in your stance, pick the club up steeply in your backswing and hit down sharply.

2 Depending on the lie, you will probably have to hold on to the club tightly through impact to stop the thick grass twisting the face into a closed position. Commit to the shot and never decelerate the clubhead through impact.

3 Make it your goal to swing through into a decent length follow-through. You may struggle to release the club, and the rough will inevitably restrict your swing, but you should always accelerate the clubhead purposefully through impact.

THE FAIRWAY BUNKER SHOT

Hitting a full shot from a fairway bunker can be a terrifying prospect for many amateur golfers. Even accomplished low handicappers and professionals will view the shot with a great deal of respect because the margin for error is tiny. If you catch the sand first when playing a shot from a bunker, the heavy resistance of the sand can stop a fast-moving clubhead stone-dead in its tracks. The end result is low swing speed and very little distance. You will be lucky to remove the ball from the bunker, let alone get it to the green.

Much depends on how high the lip on the front of the bunker is, but if the ball is lying well there is no reason why you cannot hit a fairway wood provided you keep your swing smooth and controlled.

Maintaining balance is the key to the long bunker shot. Play it as you would a long iron from a tight lie.

Address and swing

Maintaining your height, spine angle and knee flex are the keys to consistent ball striking and that philosophy is just as applicable to playing from a fairway bunker as from anywhere else, since any loss of height will cause the clubhead to dig into the sand before the ball. Keep your swing as smooth and controlled as possible while avoiding sudden changes in swing speed and lunges at the ball. That will ensure successful fairway-bunker play.

Escaping a fairway bunker

1 Your priority is to ensure that the clubhead does not make contact with the sand before the ball. Set up as though you are going to play a shot from the fairway. Avoid shuffling your feet into the sand as that will lower your body and increase your chances of catching the shot heavy. Straighten your legs slightly to raise the clubhead off the ground.

2 As you make your swing, it is important to maintain your height. Focus on keeping the flex in your knees and your spine angle consistent all the way through from start to finish. If your body bobs up and down, the shot will become very difficult.

3 With little margin for error at impact, it is a good idea to keep your rhythm and tempo as smooth and even-paced as possible. If you can avoid sudden lunges or dramatic changes in your swing speed, you will stand a much better chance of staying in control of the shot and clipping the ball neatly off the top of the sand.

THE SHORT GAME

The short irons are the ones that can really keep your scorecard looking respectable. It is no use getting up to the green in two shots if you then take three to get the ball in the hole. Confidence in your short-range shots to the green will help you turn three shots into two and even two into one.

Feeling confident is the all-important factor in honing your short game. You'll have often heard it said that golf, like many major sports, is mostly played in the mind and 90 per cent of the short game is played in the head. It is primarily about feeling sure of your short shots. That sense of confidence will come from having the correct technique to play each shot and through practising that technique until it has become second nature.

Score-saving shots

No matter how consistent a player is from tee to green, they will always find themselves chipping several times during every round. Even the best players hit only 13 to 14 greens in 'regulation' per round. This means that superstars such as Tiger Woods and Phil Mickelson regularly rely on their short game to keep their scores low.

Imagination and vision

The wide variety of courses, together with variables such as the pin position, the size, shape and contours of the putting surface and the lie of the ball, mean that there are an infinite number of shots that you can face around the greens. You have only half-a-dozen or so suitable clubs at your disposal, however, so vision and imagination play a key role in an accomplished short game. Without the ability to picture a shot in your mind, you will stand little chance of executing it successfully.

The good news is that almost anyone can improve their short game. It takes neither fantastic athleticism nor timing to hit a shot on to the green. All a player needs is a basic understanding of the technique and the desire to improve.

SEVEN-IRON TO WEDGE

The short irons comprise those clubs from the 7-iron through to the wedge. The higher the club number, the shorter the shot and the greater the need for accuracy. Any reasonably proficient player will be hoping to hit the green at least eight times out of ten with any clubs numbered seven, eight or nine. Any professional will be truly disgusted if he doesn't get the ball to within 20 feet (6 metres) of the hole with a wedge.

Seven-iron

Most beginners start out hitting shots with clubs such as the 7-iron and quickly make friends with them. The natural loft of the club means that they are straightforward to use and there is no problem getting the ball airborne. The accent is on finesse and accuracy, and the vast majority of players feel more comfortable trying to transmit those qualities with a golf club than when the accent is on power.

The maximum distance we are talking about here is 150 yards (137 metres), which is about the outer limit that a good player will expect to hit when using a 7-iron. More typically, the average amateur will hit it 130–140 yards (119–128 metres). Because it is so important that you hit the greens frequently when using your short irons, it is vital that you know just how far you hit with your 7-iron. To find out this information, do a simple yardage check (see page 41). Once you know your capabilities with a 7-iron, take ten yards off for each club of a higher denomination.

Perfect practice

Always remember that you can save many more shots practising your short game than with your long irons or driver. If your practice time is limited and you don't know whether to work on your ball striking with your woods or your technique around the greens, plump for the latter. After all, think of a player like Bernard Gallacher, who not only captained three Ryder Cup teams but also competed in eight. This was a man who was fairly unimpressive off the tee, but more than made up for it with tenacity and confidence around the greens. There's no way that he would have achieved all he did in the game if his skills had been the other way round, where he had been great off the tee, but possessed an average short game. Always practise with purpose, aiming at specific targets at known distances.

Get to know the distance each of your short irons will give you.

TECHNIQUE FOR 7- TO 9-IRONS

When using a 7-, 8- or 9-iron, there is no great change in general technique from using the longer clubs (see pages 26–31). One slight difference is that the shafts are shorter than with the long irons and so the knee bend should be a little more pronounced and the forearms more relaxed. The ball should also be positioned in your stance halfway between the middle of your feet and your left toe.

When you tee the ball up on a par three, make sure that the peg is pressed well into the ground so that only the tip of it is visible above the grass.

The backswing

Because the shafts are shorter, you will be standing closer to the ball and will have less freedom to turn your shoulders; so your backswing will inevitably not be as long as it would be with your driver. This is a good thing as the key with these shots is control and accuracy. Clearly, if your backswing is slightly shorter, then that offers more control, and more control means more accuracy.

Over-clubbing

Never try to force a short iron. You often hear of professionals hitting a 'hard' 7-iron, but if you think a shot calls for everything you've got with an 8-iron then opt for smoothness and rhythm and hit with a 7-iron. It is impossible to over-stress that the key with short irons is that distance isn't everything. Off the tee, an extra 20 yards (18 metres) might set up an easier second shot but, with a short iron, it is getting the ball close to the pin that counts. You are much more likely to achieve that with a smooth 7-iron than with a hard 8-iron.

Because a player is standing that much closer to the ball than with longer clubs, and less can go wrong owing to the shorter shaft, a player soon gains real confidence with the short irons. A few crisp, short-iron shots out of the middle of the club should help the golfing bug to bite hard.

Tee height

On shorter par threes, you will occasionally be hitting anything from a 7-iron to a wedge; something to be avoided is to tee up the ball at the normal height. For these shots, many good players will dispense with a tee altogether, on the grounds that they get more feel without one. But if you feel more comfortable with a tee, make sure it is firmly stuck in the ground and the ball nestling just the merest smidgen off the turf. Accomplished players always take a divot even when hitting a short iron off the tee. They squeeze the ball between club and turf, which imparts backspin to the ball. This enables them to stop the ball dead on the green. Hitting from a tee peg you will not get backspin and you must allow for the ball to roll after landing.

Short iron tips

1 Because you are standing nearer to the ball, your posture when hitting a short iron, such as a 9-iron, will be a little more angular than when hitting a longer iron. Otherwise, there is no major difference in the set-up.

2 As with the pitching wedge, it is unlikely that you will need to swing the club back to the horizontal. If you retain the flex and resistance in your right knee, this is about as far back as you should go.

3 Irons are designed to be struck with a slightly more descending blow than the driver and fairway woods, which require a more shallow angle of attack. Don't be afraid to hit down and through the ball and always look to take a divot.

WHEN TO USE 7- TO 9-IRONS

The vast majority of full 7- to 9-iron shots will be used to fire to greens. However, these clubs are also good trouble-shooters. Occasionally, you'll find yourself having to hit a 9-iron over trees to relocate your fairway or you will punch the ball out of woodland back on to the mown stuff by using a 7-iron.

The safe seven

The 7-iron is more likely to play a greater part in your overall decision-making process than the 9-iron. If, for example, you are playing a par five that you can reach with a driver, 3-iron and a wedge, but you don't like hitting a 3-iron and are worried that doing so will leave you in trouble, you may consider hitting a driver and then two 7-irons. The most important thing in golf is to get the job done, and if the tools you use are a little unorthodox, then so be it.

MEASURING STANCE WIDTH

The width of your stance is important for a decent swing. If your legs are too wide, you'll restrict your swing; too narrow and you'll lose control. To ensure you are not standing with your legs too far apart, use this measure.

Hold the end of two clubs and hang them from your shoulders as you take an address position. Let the clubs dangle freely and note where the clubs point. For longer irons and woods, the clubs should point at the inside of your heels.

IRON ADDRESS

With the shorter irons, as the ball comes back in your stance, your weight should be more evenly spread. You want to have a steeper angle of attack at impact, generating a slightly downward blow, as opposed to the sweeping, more shallow angle needed to hit woods.

Trees and short irons

When a tree blocks your route to the green, you have to decide whether to go over it or under it. Unless you are confident of clearing the top of the branches, punch the ball underneath instead.

If your route to the green is completely blocked by a tree, chip sideways where possible, or even take a penalty drop. Don't risk 'breaking' your hands or the club by attempting a full shot.

If your backswing is totally restricted by a tree, chip the ball out sideways and back on to the fairway.

HEAVY ROUGH AND FLYING LIES

The short irons have adequate loft to deal with heavy rough, and the rougher it is, the shorter the iron that you will need. If you are up to your neck in it, you may have to consider taking an unplayable lie (see page 112), but the general rule is that if you can see the ball, or any part of it, then a sand wedge will be able to get the ball out (see pages 86–87).

Tall rough tips

When the ball is lying in heavy rough, don't get too greedy. Getting the ball back in play first time is your priority.

Deep rough

The most important thing when playing from heavy rough is to keep your eye on the ball. The temptation is to lift the head early in order to witness your miraculous recovery shot. However, there will be no miraculous recovery shot if you do. Playing from heavy rough is one instance when you can swing the club harder than normal but not if extra power comes at the expense of rhythm. You still have to have complete control of the clubhead as there is always the danger that the ball will not budge, or not budge enough for you to relocate it on to the fairway. Take several practice swings so that you know what the rough feels like.

A steep backswing is required to hit down through the ball to remove it from the rough.

Flying lie

This is a ball situated in the first cut of rough, with a cushion of grass under the ball. That grass comes between the clubface and the ball and ends any chance a player has of imparting spin, so the ball ends up flying much farther than normal. You'll soon be able to deduce whether you have a flying lie or not. The ball feels extremely sweet off the clubface, but clearly, if it is flying 20 yards (18 metres) more or so, the final result might not be so sweet. But once you have detected a flying lie, you can make allowances and take a club less than normal if you are playing to the green.

Magic 150 yards (137 metres)

When you are looking to escape trouble and are forced to lay up, don't take the high-risk club that will get you 20 yards (18 metres) nearer the green if you are lucky. Instead, look for the 150-yard markers instead. All you need to do is be inside these – as soon as you are within 150 yards (137 metres), you have a chance of hitting it close and taking one putt, most likely two, but no worse.

TROUBLE RULES

7/10 Rule When you are eyeing up a Seve Ballesteros-esque escape shot, stop. Have a think about the shot you are attempting – is it really within your ability to shape a ball 200 yards (183 metres) around a large oak tree from the thick rough? If you think you could pull the shot off seven times out of ten, then have a go. If the odds are less, chip out sideways.

Rough
The area of unmown grass that lies either side of the fairway.

WEDGES

Two wedges will get the job done for most beginners. A pitching wedge will allow you to play not only the shots that the name suggests but also little chips from around the green. With a sand wedge you can play bunker shots, as the name of the club suggests, but this club can also be used close to the green for 'flop' shots where you need to land the ball softly on the putting surface. A third wedge – the lob wedge – can be useful for the golfers who would rather hit a full shot as often as possible.

Grip further down the shaft for fuller feel and control on pitch shots.

The pitching grip

Use your orthodox grip for the pitch shot, but grip down the shaft. This will give you more control of the clubhead and improve your feel for the shot. Usually you pitch with a pitching wedge, but if you need to play a shot that flies higher and stops quicker, use either a sand or lob wedge.

Hold the club gently – you do not want tension in your arms; they need to feel relaxed, loose and fluid, to help with touch and feel. A pitch is not as mechanical as a full shot – it is more about natural instincts and flair. But don't be so relaxed that you quit on the shot. Make sure you make a full follow-through.

Key points for accurate wedge shots

1 When hitting a wedge shot, make sure that your stance is fairly narrow. It is perfectly acceptable to aim your feet a fraction left of the target to give yourself room to swing the club through on impact.

2 The shorter length of the shaft means that it is unlikely that you will be able to reach the horizontal with a pitching wedge. But when accuracy is more important than power, there is no need.

3 Just because you are playing a fairly short-range shot, it doesn't mean you should swing slowly through the ball. Swing at your normal speed and commit fully to releasing the club, just as you would with a long iron.

4 Many amateur golfers allow their weight to fall on to their back foot through impact in an attempt to scoop the ball into the air. Let the loft on the clubface do the work and make sure that you finish with your weight on your front foot.

PITCHING

The range of a pitch shot for an amateur is from within 30–70 yards (27–64 metres) of the green. The pitch is played with a long swing and a lofted club – almost always a pitching wedge or sand wedge. The aim of this shot is to send the ball into the green fairly high, so that it stops quickly and rolls only a short distance once it lands. If executed sweetly, it is one of the most pleasing shots in golf.

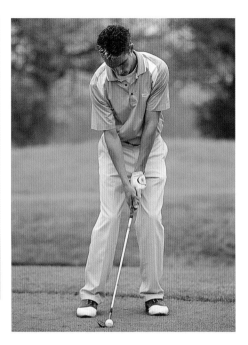

A slightly open stance encourages a steep back lift.

Timing

Professionals will aim to hit the ball to within 10 feet (3 metres) of the flag, but most amateur golfers are satisfied merely with getting the ball on to the green. Many regard a pitch of 50 yards (45 metres) from the fairway with the same trepidation as a bunker shot. The main reason for this lack of confidence is that, because the pitch requires a less than full swing, it is easy for players to lose their timing. As a result, the swing feels awkward and unnatural, but there's no magic secret to mastering this shot. The pitch simply requires an abbreviation of the normal, full swing (see pages 26–31), with a few minor adjustments to the set-up (see pages 24–25) to help reduce the distance the ball travels. Timing and tempo are the keys to consistent pitching.

You can improve your mental attitude towards pitching by viewing it as an attacking option, rather than as merely a recovery shot. Good pitching will not only help you save pars but will also help you to pick up birdies on par fives and short par fours. However, before you can land the ball on a dime from 50 yards (45 metres), you must first develop a solid technique.

The abbreviated shot

Pitching should be your major ally in your short game but although, on the face of it, a pitch shot seems an easier option than a bunker shot, many golfers struggle with their pitching because they feel uncomfortable shortening their swing. Players who are unsure how to play the shot either speed up their rhythm to compensate for their shorter backswing or swing too lazily and leave the ball short of their intended target. One thing to remember is that the pitch shot is simply an abbreviation of the full swing (see pages 26–31).

The ability to pitch the ball safely on to the green first time will help you avoid dropping shots needlessly. Many strokes are wasted from within 70 yards (64 metres) of the flag purely because the golfer cannot land the ball on the green from this distance. Instead he or she leaves the ball short and then has to rely on another chip to get the ball close to the hole.

A controlled, measured pitch can take you on to the green, regardless of the obstacles in your way.

THE PERFECT PITCH

If there are two common faults among the poor pitchers of this world, it is that they have their weight on the right-hand side in a misguided attempt to scoop the ball into the air and that their backswing is too long and they therefore decelerate through the ball. Concentrate on these two things and the days of poor pitching will soon belong to your previous life.

KEY POINTS TO REMEMBER

- Transfer weight on to your left side as you start down
- Start downswing with your left hip
- Don't start the stroke with your right shoulder or arms
- Hold your wrist hinge on way down
- At point of impact, hips are open to target, weight is on left and left knee is straight
- Release powerfully through impact and extending arms
- Make a full balanced finish

The set-up

As you are looking for accuracy rather than power with a pitch shot, bring your feet closer together, stand a little nearer the ball and choke down on the club. Some coaches recommend that you open your stance a little (aim left with your feet and hips) to give yourself room to swing the club through impact, but this is not strictly necessary. For the regular pitch shot, the ball should be played in the centre of the stance with the weight distributed evenly between the feet.

1 From the amended address position, you should make your normal swing. You must focus on maintaining a fluid rhythm as you swing your arms away. As with the full swing, the arms should remain tucked into the side of the chest and not move away from the body, and the wrists should 'break' gently, but fully.

2 As the emphasis is on accuracy rather than power, there's no need for any excessive lower body action. You should control the shot by rotating your upper body back and through. The ball is simply left to get in the way of the swing. Good tempo is necessary – if you are an anxious pitcher it is easy to fall into the trap of rushing the shot. You do not want to mollycoddle the ball towards the hole, either. Pitch shots must be played authoritatively. Watch the world's top players and you will see that they commit totally to the shot, safe in the knowledge that the narrow stance, shorter backswing and lofted club will prevent them from hitting the ball too far.

3 Avoid trying to scoop the ball up into the air. Instead, trust the loft on the clubface to get the ball airborne. Most pitch shots are fluffed when the golfer tries to scoop the ball into the air and inadvertently straightens their legs and/or upper body. When this happens, it is very easy to catch the ball thin or heavy. If you can maintain your height throughout the swing, however, you stand a good chance of making crisp contact with the ball. The length of the follow-through should mirror the length of the backswing.

JUDGING DISTANCE

Once you have mastered the basic pitching action (see pages 66–67), your next step is to enhance your distance control. Great pitching technique without control is worthless, but judging distance is probably the most difficult aspect of the short game for most amateurs. Tour professionals can constantly work on their touch and feel through daily play and practice, but the chances are that you will not have that luxury and will need a few short cuts.

Many of the top professionals rely on their feel to help them to judge the distance of their short-range shots, but for most amateurs it will help to know how far you can carry the ball using different length backswings. Using your hips, chest and shoulders as reference points will help you develop more control.

Three clubs, three swings, nine distances

One good way of improving distance control is to use three clubs for pitching: a 9-iron, a pitching wedge and a sand wedge. Starting with the sand wedge, you should make a note of how far you can carry the ball when swinging back to hip, chest and shoulder height. This gives you three different distances. You can then do the same with the pitching wedge and 9-iron, making a written or mental note of the results. At the end of this process, you will have nine different distances at your disposal.

More club choice for pitching?

As well as a pitching wedge, a sand wedge and a 9-iron, you can also use an 8-iron or a lob wedge for pitch shots, depending on how far you need to hit the ball and how quickly you need it to stop when it reaches the green. Having extra pitching clubs at your disposal means more options. For instance, if the green-front is open and turf free-running, as it might be on a links or heathland course, you might pitch with a 6- or 7-iron, running the ball most of the way on the ground.

Practise for the real thing

Many of us simply throw a bag of balls on to the practice ground, hitting them with little real purpose. We probably set each ball on a nice, new piece of turf, making life easy for ourselves. But out on the course we may have to hit from bare lies or divot holes, long grass or scrub, even through the branches of trees.

Try to practise pitching from all these situations. Play one shot imagining that you have to clear a small tree. Play the next shot to the same target, this time imagining you have to keep below the branches of a tree.

Practising pitching

1 Take your sand wedge, swing back so that your hands reach hip height. Note how far you hit the ball.

2 Now swing back to chest height and again note how far you hit the ball.

3 Swing to shoulder height and not the distance. Repeat with pitching wedge and 9-iron and you have pitch shots for nine different ranges.

PITCHING OVER A BUNKER

To pitch a ball successfully over a bunker is ten per cent technique and 90 per cent confidence. There are, however, two pitfalls that always trap the unwary beginner:

- being so worried about the shot that the player 'quits' on it, decelerating into the hitting area. Wrists go rigid and the swing stutters. The result is that he or she hits behind the ball and it trickles into the very bunker they're trying to avoid, or, even more humiliatingly, stops short and they have then got the same shot to play over again;

- the player is so worried about the shot that they're looking to see where it has finished even before they've completed the backswing. The result is that they 'thin' it and the ball flies past the target at great speed, invariably leaving the player in a similar predicament over the other side of the green.

Fear and loft

Clearly the key that links both these pitching shots is the fear of botching it up. The bunker is no longer just a hazard but a snarling menace, with an insatiable desire for your golf ball. Another common failing is the worry that the club does not possess enough loft to get the ball over the sand, so the player tries to scoop it over. Nothing could more certainly lead to failure. Before playing the shot, take several practice swings, concentrating on only taking the club back to the horizontal and following-through the same amount.

Key points on pitching

1 When you need to get the ball up in the air quickly, open your stance at address and play the ball towards your front foot.

Technique

First things first when pitching over a bunker: make sure your technique is correct. The ball should be set in the middle of your stance and the weight should slightly favour the left-hand side. The most important aspects now are control and rhythm. The best way to ensure the former is with a backswing restricted to half your normal length – any more than that and you're asking for trouble. The follow-through will almost certainly be about the same length if you have mastered the rhythm. Swing normally. Think smooth and keep your legs still. Let the club do the work – it will have more than enough loft to get the ball over the bunker.

Also think half and half: half a backswing and half a follow-though. The swing should involve a slight acceleration through the ball, but not so much that it disturbs your rhythm. That is all-important. If you're ever at a professional tournament, just wander over to the practice ground and watch the professionals working on this shot. One thing will quickly be apparent: their half-swings all possess the same tempo and all are as smooth as silk.

2 To create extra height on the shot, pick the club up fairly steeply with your hands and wrists as soon as you can in your backswing.

3 To maximize the loft on the clubface and to generate height on the ball, keep the grooves on the clubhead facing the sky through impact and well into your follow-through.

DIVOT AND LIE PLAY

DIVOT

With luck you will never have to face playing a pitch shot from a divot. But sometimes you will play a course where there is a hole that leaves you a pitch shot of 40 yards (36 metres) over water. Here you might find a gathering of divots and your ball may well finish in one of them.

A controlled pitch

By all means, take a couple of seconds to curse your luck, but this is really another shot that looks worse than it is. Once more, adopt your normal stance for a pitch shot:

- the ball in the middle of your feet;

- your weight predominantly on your left side;

- your shoulders and feet slightly open to the target.

Your object here is for the club to meet the back of the ball just before taking a smidgen of turf, and the best way for you to do this is with a controlled half backswing, leading to a smooth acceleration through the ball. Once you've successfully completed this shot you will be surprised how much of the fear has evaporated the next time.

When your ball is on a bare lie or in a divot, the situation can often look worse than it actually is. Think calmly, and logically work through the movements involved to create a successful pitch.

It is a rule of etiquette associated with the game of golf that every player should replace their divots. However, this isn't always the case, and you may need help to achieve the shot well.

BARE LIES

A pitch shot from a bare lie is much more common than one where your ball has unluckily trundled into a divot. Even on the best links courses, the ground around the bunkers near the greens can get very parched. Many amateurs dread playing a pitch shot over a bunker from a bare lie.

The professionals, however, would much rather face such a scenario than a cushioned lie because it enables them to impart spin on the ball. Once again this is a shot where basic technique will help you overcome any fears – the normal pitch shot rules apply (see pages 66–67).

Playing from a bare lie

1 It's imperative that you set up with your hands ahead of the ball at address to ensure a crisp strike. The last thing you want is for the clubhead to bounce off the ground into the back of the ball.

2 Through impact, make sure that your hands return to exactly the same position that they occupied at address – a couple of inches (5 cm) ahead of the ball.

CHIPPING

A chip shot is played from around the edge of the green and is intended to loft the ball over the longer 'fringe' grass or rough and on to the putting surface. Once a chip shot reaches the green, the ball should roll gently the rest of the way along the ground just like a putt. The aim is to put the ball close enough to the hole to leave a very short putt. Many top professionals are such expert chippers that they are often disappointed if they don't hole-out the shot.

The lofted putt

One of the reasons that the top pros are so confident is that they treat the chip shot as an extension of their putting stroke. Many players even use their putting grip to play the shot. The idea is to get the ball running as soon as possible, so a neat and compact stroke with very little hand action is best. Only rarely will a top professional loft the ball high into the air from around the green. The best players know that it is easier to judge the shot and control the ball when it's rolling along the ground.

Some players have a favourite club that they use to play the majority of their shots around the green, but most will use anything from a 4-iron to a sand wedge, depending on how far they are from the hole and how much rough they need to clear first. You should

Confidence in your technique leads to flair and imagination around the greens.

use a variety of clubs for chips while you strive to learn how the ball reacts off the clubface of any given club and to judge the speed of the resultant shot.

Confidence

Chipping should be relatively simple (see pages 76–77). The technique is not as complex as a full-swing, the distances are not as large. So why is it so troublesome? If you are confident, your technique will be solid, your thoughts positive and your ball-striking will be clean. How many times do you see professional golfers chip the ball close when they are around the green? They never seem to miss and they roll the ball to within a couple of feet (0.5 metres) every time. They never mess up the shot so that it dribbles only a yard (metre), or catch the top of the ball, 'thinning' it through the back of the green.

The best chippers in the world, such as Seve Ballesteros, complement exemplary technique with awesome imagination. They can not only play the most incredible shots but they can also see them in their minds before they hit the ball. This is a great skill that you too can develop through practice and experience.

Understanding the ball's reaction

Standing on a green lobbing balls with your hands, just to see how they react on the putting surface, is a great way of nurturing imagination. A positive attitude will also help: look to hole your chips as opposed simply to getting them close. You'll soon stop worrying about fluffing these shots and will be free to use your imagination as much as possible.

Chipping requires precision and a delicacy of touch.

BASIC CHIPPING PRINCIPLES

The basic chip is one of golf's most simple shots. The swing is short – back and through – yet, despite its simplicity, many golfers mess up this shot. There are three main reasons for this:

- the player tries to add extra loft to the clubface by scooping the ball into the air. Most likely the ball will be thinned;

- the player stubs the clubhead into the ground behind the ball. Top players lead the clubface with their hands. This guarantees a crisp strike and ensures that the ball stays low to the ground;

- lack of acceleration through impact. Many golfers make a good backswing, then completely quit on the shot. With a fairly short swing, players must keep the clubhead accelerating smoothly through the ball. Loss of speed leads to loss of control.

Technique

1 To ensure your chipping set-up is geared towards control and accuracy, shuffle your feet fairly close together and, keeping the ball just behind centre in a slightly open stance, ease your weight on to the front foot so that you lean towards the target. By following this routine you will set your hands ahead of the clubface and the ball.

2 Keeping your weight on the left side, swing the club away with your arms and shoulders. It's perfectly acceptable for the wrists to 'break' a little in response to the weight of the club, but you shouldn't try to 'break' them intentionally. The backswing should be compact.

3 Assuming that you have kept your weight on the left side throughout the swing, your hands should automatically return to their address position and lead the clubface through impact. You should feel as though you are hitting down on the ball with a descending blow. This action is the key to imparting a little backspin on the ball.

4 Stay down through the shot and wait until you have struck the ball before looking up to see where it has gone. Make sure your hands remain ahead of the clubface well into the follow-through.

CHIPPING PRACTICE AND STRATEGY

Never be afraid to experiment with your short game in as imaginative and creative a fashion as you wish. Trying out different shots on the practice ground will help you find out what is possible and, just as importantly, what is not. Knowing how the ball will react with different clubs and from different lies is invaluable. You should use all the tools in your bag when chipping, even if they seem unconventional. If you are in the fringe around the green and the grass is likely to snag your club, avoid this by chipping with a 3- or 5-wood. Nor should you be afraid to use your putter in strange places – this is often the best option for a percentage shot provided there are not any obstacles in your path.

Using different clubs

By experimenting with your different clubs you will find that no two chip shots are the same and this fact means your ability to judge distance and to select the correct club is absolutely vital. As you practise chipping with a selection of clubs, you will get used to the carry and roll of each iron (see table, below). Using the same length of swing, a shot played with a 5-iron, for example, will carry farther and roll more on landing than one played with a pitching wedge, which will hit the ball higher into the air and stop it quicker. Some leading golfers, including Tiger Woods, occasionally play shots from the fringe around the green with a 3-wood, where an iron club might snag in the grass resulting in a fluffed shot.

Carry
The distance from when a ball is struck to when it first lands.

THE RATIO OF CARRY AND ROLL WITH DIFFERENT CLUBS

Club	Carry	Roll
Sand wedge	90%	10%
Pitching wedge	80%	20%
9-iron	70%	30%
8-iron	60%	40%
7-iron	50%	50%
6-iron	40%	60%
5-iron	30%	70%
4-iron	20%	80%
3-iron	10%	90%

Use the clock face to gauge your chips.

Always make a positive through-swing.

SAFETY FIRST

When playing a chip shot, you should aim to get the ball on the green and rolling towards the hole as soon as possible. Unless there is no other option, you should avoid trying to run the ball through rough or long fringe grass, as it is impossible to know how the ball will react. It could get a nice bounce and run on to the hole without any problems, but it could just as easily get snagged and caught up in the longer grass, leaving you to face yet another chip shot. To be on the safe side, you should try to carry the ball a yard (metre) or so on to the green.

When chipping, aim to get the ball on the green and running towards the hole as soon as possible.

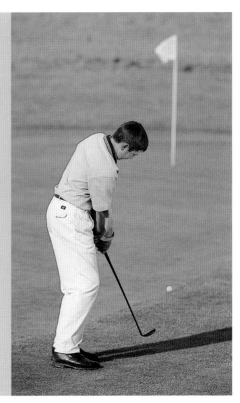

MAKING YOUR CHIP SHOTS

Once you know what ratio of carry and roll you can expect with each club (see page 78), making your shots becomes easier. All you need decide is which club will loft the ball on to the green and still produce enough roll to get it to the hole. If your ball is just a couple of feet (0.5 metres) off the green, a straighter-faced chipping club will pop it over the fringe and enable it to roll the rest of the way. However, if you are farther away, you will need a more lofted club; exactly which one depends on how far you are from the green and, from there, the distance to the hole.

Paying attention
Read chips like putts, look to hole your chip shots and always visualize the shot before playing it. Make plenty of practice strokes while looking at the target to enhance your sense of distance and, finally, commit to the shot. Watch the behaviour of the ball once it has landed. It will tell you a lot about your next putt, especially if the ball goes beyond the hole.

Lofted chips
Chip shots, which stay low to the ground, are preferable in many situations but there are times when such 'safe' shots are not an option. For example, when the pin is cut close to the front edge and there is a lot of rough to carry, a high, 'floating' shot may offer the only chance of getting the ball close to the hole.

Visualizing your shot

1 The world's top golfers actively look to hole their chip shots and you should be just as positive. Pay as much attention to a chip as you would to a putt. You need to read the break and borrow on the greens.

The first thing you must do when playing a lofted shot is to check the lie. If the ground is dry or bare, you should forget it, as the leading edge of the clubface will bounce off the ground and into the back of the ball. The result will be a shot that races across the green. You should attempt to play this shot only if you can get the clubface under the ball. You can get extra loft by opening the club face a little. Do this by turning the club out as you grip. Don't do it by turning your hands. The ball will fly to the right of the target line, so aim a little left of the target.

2 When planning your chip shot, it's a good idea to walk to a point roughly halfway between the ball and the hole to get a better perspective of the distance. You will also be able to see how the ball will 'break' nearer to the flag.

3 Once you have assessed the break and the line of the shot, make several practice swings – ideally while looking at the hole – to get a feel for the length of backswing you will need to get the ball to the hole.

4 Once you have finished your pre-shot preparation, trust your initial instincts and commit to playing the shot as you planned and visualized it. Never quit on the ball through impact.

THE DOWNHILL CHIP

When playing from any kind of sloping lie, either on the fairway or around the green, you should set up with your shoulders parallel to the ground. That way you effectively recreate a flat lie, which will enable you to play the shot using only a slightly adapted version of the normal swing (see pages 26–31). Another secret is knowing how the slope will affect the flight of the ball. The downhill chip is very tricky as the ball shoots off the clubface low and fast.

Keep your balance

It is a natural instinct to fight the slope. Your body wants to shift your weight uphill. Take several practice strokes, keeping your weight consistently on the front foot, with your head still and your shoulders parallel with the slope. Reproduce the same feelings as you play the shot for real.

Technique

1 When you set your shoulders parallel to the ground on a downslope, your weight will automatically fall on to the front foot. This is not a problem, but you should widen your stance a fraction to provide extra stability. You will also need to play the ball a little further forward to compensate for the fact that your weight is on the left side. In addition, you may want to lower the grip by about 1 inch (2.54 cm) or so to get more control over the shot.

2 To avoid swinging straight back into the slope, you will probably have to 'break' your wrists a little earlier than normal (see pages 26–31). Keeping your weight on the left side, swing the club away with your arms. This action will feel as though you are picking the club up steeply in the backswing with your wrists.

3 The clubhead should stay as low to the ground as possible in the downswing. You should feel as though you are reaching down for the ball with your arms extended. The clubhead should trace the contours of the slope and slide under the ball.

4 To guard against trying to scoop the ball into the air, keep the clubhead low to the ground well into the follow-through. Try to have the arms extended for as long as possible to ensure that the clubhead slides underneath the ball and follows the contours of the ground.

BUNKERS

In 1932, Gene Sarazen came up with the perfect solution for his weakness out of bunkers – he invented the sand wedge. He knew the reason for his poor play was that the niblick (wedge) wasn't designed to get underneath the ball, taking a layer of sand, so he put a flange on the back of it.

'I spent hours practising that shot and getting the flange just right and it got so I would bet even money I could get down in two out of sand,' Sarazen recalled, years later. In 1935, he became the first player to win all four major championships at least once, a feat that only other four players – Ben Hogan, Jack Nicklaus, Gary Player and Tiger Woods – have since emulated.

Conquering the fear

The sand wedge may now be available to golfers of every standard but that has not yet prevented bunkers inducing a sinking feeling in many players every time their ball veers, often agonisingly slowly but inevitably, into a bunker. It can be infuriating to watch the top players regularly splash the ball from the sand to within a yard (metre) of the flag, especially when you tend to write off at least a couple of shots when you land in a bunker.

Bunkers are not, though, the evil monsters they might first appear. Once you get the hang of them you may prefer to have a sand shot than a chip from a fluffy lie, because you can get more control and spin from a bunker. Firstly, though, you have to get out.

Controlling your 'escape'

Although you may be able to escape a sand trap in one shot, you may have absolutely no idea where the ball will finish. Sometimes it flies 20 feet (6 metres) past the flag; at other times it just creeps out, landing 10 feet (3 metres) short. You may also knock it dead once in a while. This is frustrating but can easily be put right with a couple of technical checks and some practice. Finding touch and feel out of the bunkers comes from solid technique.

Remember that out of every shot in golf, the standard bunker shot is one of the most forgiving. You don't hit the ball, but the sand behind it, and the equipment is specially designed for the shot so that, if used properly, you'll escape almost regularly. So attack this hazard positively.

THE SAND WEDGE

One of the main reasons that top professionals are so confident about playing from a bunker is that they understand how to take advantage of the design of the sand wedge in order to make the shot easier.

The anatomy of a sand wedge

Take a close look at the base of a sand wedge and you will notice that, unlike the rest of the irons, it has a wide sole. You will also see that the back of the club is set slightly lower than the leading edge of the clubface. This feature is called the 'bounce' and enables the wide part of the sole, rather than the thin leading edge, to make contact with the sand. The clubhead is, therefore, literally able to bounce through the sand taking a thin, shallow divot. The bounce angle becomes even more noticeable if the clubface is opened up. A skilful golfer will vary the angle of the clubface to create shots of different heights and trajectories.

A bunker is considered a hazard and, therefore, the clubhead must never touch the sand at address. If the clubface touches the sand prior to a swing, the player will incur a two-shot penalty. Also, unless there is a local rule to the contrary, players are not permitted to remove stones or other loose impediments.

Swing across the target line

One confusing aspect of bunker play is that players are told to open their stance at address and to swing across the target line from out to in. The reason for this is that the address position takes its lead from the design of the sand wedge. When the clubface is opened to make full use of the 'bounce' on the sole, the club aims to the right, so, to compensate, the player must aim left. All golfers must understand the

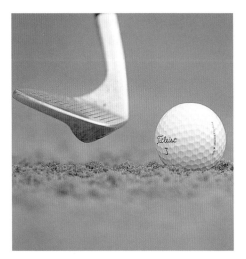

The sand wedge is designed specially to ease the ball out of a bunker.

need to swing along the line of their feet and shoulders, no matter how strange it feels. Don't forget, the club aims right, the player aims left, and the ball flies straight. Remember to hit down. Don't try to scoop the ball out of the sand.

THE GOLDEN RULE – NO BALL/CLUB CONTACT

The sand wedge is a unique club not only because it is designed for a specific purpose but also because it should never actually touch the ball. You may have heard television commentators refer to a greenside bunker shot as an 'explosion' shot. The reason for this is that the objective is not to strike the ball with the clubface but to propel it out of the bunker on a thin cushion of sand. In effect, the player creates a mini-explosion by hitting approximately 1 inch (2.54 cm) behind the ball. The theory is simple: if the golfer can remove the sand from the bunker, they will remove the ball, too.

Swing across the target line and take some sand to hit a perfect bunker shot.

PLAYING THE SPLASH SHOT

As well as aligning your body slightly to the left of the target for a standard splash or greenside bunker shot (see pages 86–87), you should open your stance slightly for a medium-length bunker shot, and increase the angle to play shots from shorter range and with greater height.

You will also need to shuffle your feet 1 inch (2.54 cm) or so down into the sand to give yourself a more stable footing, enabling you to stand on the harder base level of sand rather than the fluffier top layer. Shuffling your feet down also lowers your whole body and, in turn, the base point of your swing. Consequently, the clubhead will enter the sand and slide right underneath the ball. Finally, you should remember to play the ball just forward of centre (in relation to the line of your swing, not the target line) in your stance.

The splash shot swing

Once you have made the necessary amendments to your address position, you have done most of the hard work. Playing the shot is no different to any other. However, you must remind yourself of the need to swing along the line of your feet and shoulders. All your hard work at address will count for nothing if, instead of swinging along the line of your body, you decide to swing the club along the ball-target line. This will cause you problems because your swing will then be too flat in relation to your body alignment. How far left you aim depends on the distance you want to hit the ball.

Playing a standard splash shot

1 Aim the clubface directly at, or slightly right of, the target while your feet, hips and shoulders all align to the left. Shuffle your feet into the sand for a firm footing and to lower the base point of your swing.

2 Play the ball forward in your stance so that you have plenty of room to splash the clubhead down into the sand behind the ball. Your stance should also be fairly wide to give yourself a solid base to your swing and to lower your body at address.

3 Swing back along the line of your body, maintaining a smooth and even tempo, while keeping your weight evenly balanced between both feet. Allow your wrists to hinge naturally in response to the momentum and the weight of the clubhead. Good rhythm is vital for bunker shots. Always make a full backswing.

4 Swing the club back down to the ball along the same path as the backswing and splash the clubface down into the sand. Allow the bounce and loft on the clubface to do all the work. Commitment is crucial as the heavy sand can stop a slow-moving swing dead. Accelerate the clubhead through impact.

5 One sure sign of a good splash shot is a full follow-through. If you can make it through to a full finish like this, with your weight on your front foot, then it is highly likely that you have accelerated the clubhead confidently through the sand and removed the ball with it.

ADVANCED BUNKER SHOTS

Straightforward bunker play can be difficult enough (see pages 86–87), but there are also times when the ball doesn't find a nice, clean lie in the sand. Unfair as it may seem, dealing with such shots is as much a part of the game as playing from perfect lies, so you must learn to cope with these situations, too. One thing you will quickly realize is that awkward lies arise more frequently than perfect ones.

The uphill shot against the lip

When a ball runs into a bunker at a fast pace, very often it ends up on a slight upsweep against the lip. The lie looks intimidating, but it's not as bad as it seems. Firstly, the upslope acts as a launch pad for the shot, which means that getting the ball out first time should not be too difficult. Secondly, because of the extra height generated by the shot, a positive swing can be used and you can be safe in the knowledge that the ball won't run too far.

Uphill bunker shot

1 At address, the shoulders should be set parallel to the slope. This will cause your weight to fall on to the back foot. The clubface must remain square or slightly open to the target.

2 To generate enough forward momentum on the shot, a fairly long backswing is needed. Your weight must remain on the back foot throughout the backswing.

WET SAND

After long spells of rain, the sand in a bunker will be wet and hard and will exhibit different properties than under normal circumstances. When you step into the bunker and go to take your stance, you will be able to gauge how hard the sand is. If it has not compacted, then a sand wedge will probably be the most suitable club, because the flange at the bottom of this club has been designed for use under circumstances that will prevail at least 90 per cent of the time.

However, if the sand has compacted, then the flange will bounce off it and you will hit the ball without being able to get underneath it. The result will be a thinned shot into the face of the bunker – either that or a thinned shot that clears the face of the bunker and finishes in a hedge or on another fairway. By contrast, the thinner leading edge of the pitching wedge will allow you to cut through the compacted sand and play a bunker shot in the orthodox way. The only difference is that the pitching wedge hasn't as much loft and so the ball will come out on a flatter trajectory and will roll farther.

Although you should play most bunker shots with your sand wedge, when the sand is wet and compacted a better option is your pitching wedge, which has less bounce on the sole.

3 Take about 1 inch (2.54 cm) of sand before the ball and give the ball a good, hard thump on impact. The upslope and the resistance of the sand will stop you from hitting the ball too far.

4 The upslope of the bunker will restrict the follow-through, so don't expect to see a full finish position.

Unplugging a buried lie

Although this shot looks nasty, it is not as difficult as it appears. All the player needs to do is reverse every principle that applies to the standard splash shot (see pages 88–89). Whereas a normal bunker shot is one of controlled delicacy, unplugging a buried lie requires a more forceful approach. Top players will occasionally adopt a more subtle approach, but for youngsters the aim is simply to get the ball out of the bunker and safely on to the green at the first attempt.

Playing a buried lie

1 With this shot it is the leading edge that digs into the sand. The clubface is closed and the ball is played back towards the middle of the feet. To create the steep downward attack into the ball, put most of your weight on the left side.

2 To pre-set a steep attack into the ball, 'break' your wrists immediately in the backswing. You must feel as though you are lifting the club straight up and swinging back to at least shoulder height.

3 With your weight on the left side, accelerate the clubhead down into the sand, making sure that the leading edge of the clubface makes contact with the sand first. Depending on how deeply the ball is buried, the resistance of the sand will prevent a full follow-through. The ball will come out low, fast and with little spin. Consequently, it will roll a long way once it hits the green, so plan the shot carefully.

SHALLOW-FACED BUNKER

Many players automatically reach for a sand wedge when their ball lands in a bunker, even if the trap has little or no lip to it. Their reasoning is, 'I am in sand, therefore, logically, it must call for me to use a sand wedge.' Maybe it does, but before you play your shot, think a little. If the ball is lying well in sand that is not of the fluffy kind that will stop the ball rolling, why not use a putter?

After all, what is to stop you? If the lip is low enough it will not stop the ball coming out, and if the sand is firm then the ball will roll. One thing to remember, of course, is that you will not be able to ground your putter behind the ball, just as you cannot ground your sand wedge in a bunker prior to impact.

If using a putter out of the sand, however, remember that you need to hit the ball considerably harder than normal. Don't go to extremes and thrash at it as you would a driver but allow for the fact that, even if the sand is hard, it will slow the ball. So imagine that you are putting under the same resistance as if you were putting on your back lawn – always presuming, of course, that your back lawn is neither a bowling green nor untamed.

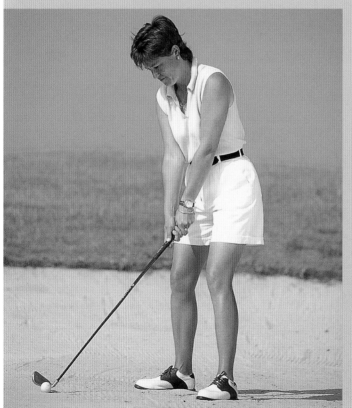

The fairway bunker holds no fears for this golfer. Her head is still, her weight is evenly distributed and her hands are slightly ahead of the clubhead all in preparation of a clean, crisp strike that will 'pick' the ball off the sand.

PUTTING

One frustrating aspect of golf is when you find the putting surface with your approach shot, then drop a shot through sloppy putting. You can hit the ball well but a string of three-putts will destroy your round. What's more, three-putting is contagious. Once you have had one or two in a row, your nerve goes and the next shot of 10 feet (3 metres) looks like 50 feet (15 metres).

All about judgement

The main reasons for three-putting are caused by misjudging line or pace. To ensure a two-putt at worst from a range of 10 feet (3 metres), line is more important than pace. If you judge the line correctly and are positive with the stroke, you should hole a few and never let one slip by.

Putting does not require any great athleticism, hand–eye coordination or strength; all that is needed is a good understanding of the technique and a feel for distance. If you can devote as much time to working on your putting as you do to your long game, you will greatly improve your handicap. Around half the shots you play during a round of golf are on the green. Developing confidence on the greens is crucial to your success as a golfer and you should continually refine your skills in this area of the game.

Good putting is a chain reaction that starts as soon as you read the putt.

Starting with a review of the putting address position (see pages 96–97) and grip (see pages 100–101), you will learn a green-reading routine (see pages 104–105), develop a consistent putting stroke (see pages 98–99) and improve your feel for distance from long range and your ability to hole-out successfully from close to the hole (see pages 106–107).

The speed of greens

Judging pace on the greens can be tricky, particularly if you are playing different courses regularly. When faced with a long putt, 20 feet (6 metres) and farther, your main priority is to gauge the pace. If you can hit the putt the right distance, you will always be close. You are not expecting to hole-out regularly from this distance, so making the ball reach the hole and stop within 2 feet (60 cm) is more important than a slight left-to-right break in the middle of the putt.

THE PUTTING SET-UP

It is often said that there is more room for individuality in putting than in any other area of the game. However, although you see a variety of weird and wonderful putting styles demonstrated successfully in professional golf, you must remember that the top players have developed an enhanced sense of touch through experience and regular practice. If your quirky stroke with all its glorious idiosyncrasies serves you well, do not change a thing, but if you are prone to bouts of inconsistency then it is probably time to give your putting stroke an overhaul, starting with a review of the basics.

The basics

Putting is not rocket science. It involves hitting the ball along the ground using a fairly short stroke, back and through. As with the full swing, your putting routine starts by aiming the club carefully at your intended line. Once you have done that correctly, you can then build the rest of your stance around the alignment of the putter face.

Before you address the ball

1 First you must read the putt. Take your first look as you arrive on the green, gauging a general idea for the putt, then look at the putt from at least two angles, usually from behind the hole and behind the ball. You should have a good idea of the break by the time you are finished.

2 Take some practice swings from behind the ball, keeping an eye on the hole as you do. Try to picture in your mind the ball travelling up the break you have chosen and into the hole. When you have got a clear image in your mind's eye, stand up to the ball.

Putting basics

1 Posture is as important in putting as it is in the long game. Stand relatively tall and create sharp angles with your spine and legs so that your arms can hang freely from your shoulders. For maximum consistency, your forearms and the putter should form a straight line.

2 To give yourself the best possible view of the line of the putt, your eyes need to be directly over the ball. You can check this by dropping another ball from the top of your nose or by hanging your putter vertically from your eyes to see if it covers the ball. Forearms and putter should form a straight line.

3 The putter face should stay low to the ground during the stroke. To avoid hitting down too steeply through impact, play the ball just forward of your sternum (chest bone), as this is just beyond the base point of the stroke and will, therefore, enable you to make contact with the ball slightly on the upswing, which is essential for imparting top spin. Top spin is vital in helping the ball roll smoothly across the putting surface.

Green
an area of closely-mown grass prepared for putting.

GENERAL TECHNIQUE

Bobby Locke, Billy Casper and Isao Aoki, to pick three players from different generations, would all have had the book thrown at them if there was only one way to putt. The fact that they were three of the best putters of all time fully illustrates that anything goes in putting if it's legal and it works.

Idiosyncrasies of style

Aoki may have had the worst style. The manual tells you that the putter head should lie square on the ground, but the toe of Aoki's putter hung proudly in the air, as if it was gasping for breath. The manual tells you that the wrists should be firm throughout the stroke; Aoki so cocked his wrists it was as though he was playing a backhand at tennis. If you had seen the young Aoki on the practice putting green, you would have told him to start again from scratch – unless you had already seen him holing putts from all over the place.

There's one player with an unorthodox putting style at every club, too, and maybe more than one; golfers who defy conventional putting laws, yet consistently hole-out from every area of the green. To a certain extent, then, putting is God-given: that seems to be the lesson here. But for the less gifted among us, there are rules that ought to be followed for consistency in this infuriating area of the sport.

There are perhaps just two basic tenets to putting:

- the wrists should stay firm throughout the stroke;
- the stroke itself should be smooth and rhythmical – it is often compared to the pendulum movement on a grandfather clock, and that is probably the best analogy of all.

Another thing to remember is that the rest of the body should remain perfectly still throughout the putting stroke. That is not to say that you should be thinking you are a statue and freeze on the spot; if you are at all tense, your putting will almost certainly go to pot. When you are about to stand over a putt, try to relax your body and then concentrate your mind on the ball, moving your arms as if they were that pendulum. Once you have mastered that, the hard part begins – learning to read the greens and the different borrows (see pages 102–103), as well as coping with the psychology at work whenever you step on to the green.

Using the putter

1 Since a putt spends all its time on the ground, there is no need for any wrist action in the stroke. Set up with your eyes over the ball, which should be played just forward of centre in your stance. The shaft of the club and your arms should form a 'Y' shape.

2 Keep the clubhead low to the ground as you swing the putter away with your arms and shoulders. Don't hinge your wrists at all and keep your head steady and your lower body still.

3 Always accelerate the putter purposefully through the ball. Never flick at the ball with your wrists to set it rolling. Simply allow it to get in the way of your rhythmical stroke.

THREE WELL-KNOWN PUTTING GRIPS

Given that putting is often considered a game within a game, it is appropriate that a little playing around with the accepted wisdom is allowed here. No-one is going to stand opposite you, studying your grip on the greens and tut-tutting, 'Well I'm sorry this will not do', as they might if they spotted something awry on a shot from the tee.

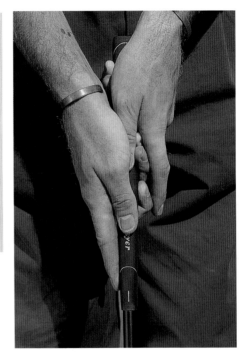

Choosing a grip

There's never been a golfer born who has not struggled at some point to get the ball in the hole and experimented as a result with different methods in an effort to find the key. In the end, however, many golfers settle on two of the methods described here. The third illustrates the boundless possibilities of putting.

And now there is a wide variety of putters, some with long handles (belly and broom-handle), others with weird and wonderful designs, and yet others with many styles of grip. Many of these call for modifications of the usual grip.

Orthodox grip

This grip is used by most players from tee to green. Perhaps they're working on the principle that it took them long enough to feel comfortable with this method without trying to get used to another one. Alternatively, they may have decided that if it's working from tee to green, they should use it on the green as well. There's certainly an obvious logic to using an orthodox grip.

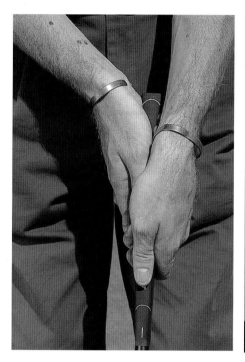
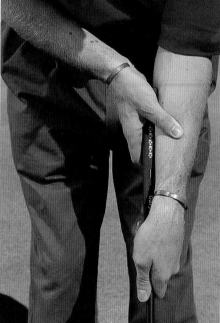

Reverse overlap

What every golfer is after is the feel of the hands being in control of the putter head. Instead of the left index finger forming an interlocking grip, many players find that by placing it over the fingers of the right hand, as here, they can achieve this feel, because the grip is now less rigid. This is perhaps the most popular method of all and one used by a number of top professionals.

The 'Langer'

The third photograph illustrates what can only be described as the Langer method. It may look interesting, but be warned; the German only alighted on this drastic solution after three bouts of the putting 'yips' and following experiments with various other methods. Langer now uses a long-handled putter.

READING GREENS

Once you have mastered the general technique of putting (see pages 98–99) and settled on a method that promotes feel (see pages 100–101), the next thing to conquer is how to understand the contours of the green and how these and the grass quality will affect your putting. Reading a green is one of golf's great challenges. You are unlikely to face exactly the same putt twice, and you are also unlikely to find a totally flat green, so the ability to read a green accurately is vital. In most cases, you will need to aim either to the right or left of the hole in order to allow for the 'break', or 'borrow'.

Assessing 'borrow'

This skill is gained more by experience than anything else. If you play most of your golf at the same course then you will learn over time the subtleties that exist on those particular greens and will master them. If a borrow stands between your ball and the hole, then the ball will deviate from a straight path because of the slope of the green, and allowances will have to be made according to its severity.

Weather conditions

The better the greens the more allowance that has to be made for borrow. Wet and windy conditions can also make quite a difference to putting. If the greens are sodden then the borrows will not have nearly the same effect as if they are dry. As a rough guide, allow perhaps half the borrow you would normally.

The hard and fast rule to observe is that the golf ball will always follow Newton's laws. So if you are putting downhill or downwind, it is going to travel much faster than in the opposite direction. The difference can be quite dramatic when the putt is both downhill and downwind. Approach such putts with extreme caution.

Reading greens well is a skill that comes with experience of playing on a variety of different courses in all weather conditions.

Cut grass

Many beginners are always puzzled as to why a top professional studies a putt from all angles, assessing it from behind the hole and also back behind the ball, and occasionally side-on as well. What they are trying to assess, in addition to the borrows, is the direction of the grain of the grass. If you are studying the putt from behind your ball and the grass looks shiny, then this means the grain is with you and the putt will be quicker than if the grass has a matt finish, which means the grain is against.

Many top golfers, particularly Americans, plum-bob to read greens. This involves hanging the putter vertically in line with the centre of the hole to see which side is higher and, therefore, how the ball will 'break'.

You'll be pleased to know that greens these days are invariably cut not just in parallel lines but across too, in order to gain a greater consistency and lessen the importance of grain. So don't lose any sleep over it. In hot climates, it's not uncommon to find the grain of the grass changes direction as the sun moves.

GREEN-READING ROUTINES

It is one thing to strike the putts correctly and have a good idea of distance. But the ball will still not regularly fall into a small hole unless you follow a regular green-reading routine.

Developing judgement

Deciding on the line and speed of a putt is something at which the top pros excel, but it is a skill that develops only with the experience of playing on a variety of courses in different conditions. Regular practice on different greens will accelerate the learning process.

To develop long-term consistency in green-reading skills, it is important to run through a specific routine as you prepare for a putt. Only by viewing each putt from the same angle, and by making the same number of practice strokes each time, will you be able to obtain consistent feedback on your judgement.

Your first steps

You should not spend too much time on your reading, though, as this can hold up the pace of play. So start to view the green as you walk on to it. You cannot afford to wait until you are standing on a green to start reading a putt. It is often difficult to detect the contours of the putting surface when standing on it, so you should, instead, start to notice the greens as soon as they are within pitching range. In many cases, you will get a better overall picture from slightly farther away, where you can see the entire green and the lie of the surrounding land.

Size up your putt calmly and carefully.

Routine putting observations

1 Putts should be viewed first from behind the ball and then from behind the hole. This approach gives you the best chance of predicting the way in which the ball will move across the putting surface. By looking from behind the hole, in addition to the standard view from behind the ball, you gain a different perspective of the undulations of the green.

2 For long putts, you should walk to a point halfway between the ball and the hole on its lowest side. This position is particularly useful as distance is best gauged from a central point, while the severity of the slope is best judged from a low vantage point.

3 Remember to follow your pre-shot routine, making a practice stroke while looking at the hole to enhance your hand-eye coordination. Let your eyes compute the distance.

4 The putter should be aimed at the intended target line – not necessarily at the hole. The feet and body should then be aligned square to that line.

PUTTING STRATEGY

It is well worth taking time to plan your putt. More often than not, however, a player will fail to do this; instead he or she will take only a quick look at the hole before making a stroke. At the other end of the scale, the top professionals are very careful about the way in which they analyze their putts. They know that mistakes on the greens can be very costly, so they give all their putts maximum concentration. They also take several practice strokes; not vague swishes with the putter but precise reproductions of the shot they are about to play. They are rehearsing the feel of the shot, at the same time visualizing the way the ball will roll to the hole.

Pace before line

Most disappointing three-putts are caused not by poor accuracy but by leaving the ball well short of the hole with the first approach putt. Even relative novices will rarely miss a putt of 4 feet (1.2 metres), but all too often players leave the ball farther than that from the hole after their first putt. Therefore, with long putts your strategy should be to remember that pace is more important than line (unlike with short putts). If the speed of a putt is good, you can afford to misjudge the line by a couple of feet (0.5 metres) and still leave yourself with a simple enough tap-in for your next shot.

Good judgement of pace is more important than line on lengthy putts.

Use the logo

Aim the logo on the ball at the line for improved accuracy. An excellent way to aim your putter face correctly is to mark your ball and then turn it so that the manufacturer's logo points directly towards the intended line. Now all you must do is set the putter face square to the logo and complete the stance. Once you have lined up, you can go ahead and make a smooth, confident stroke.

Positive put-aways

Your short-putt strategy should be to take the break out of play. All too often, missed putts from 3 to 4 feet (0.9–1.2 metres) are caused by a lack of confidence. Players frequently make the mistake of trying to 'trickle' in shots that need to be played with a positive putting stroke. Two of the world's best putters, Tiger Woods and Colin Montgomerie, knock in the short putts with a firm stroke. This method means that all you need to worry about on a short putt is the initial line, because after that you know that the ball won't have time to 'break'.

Line up with your ball's logo.

Knock short putts in firmly.

RULES & ETIQUETTE

Back in 1744, when a group of men from the Honourable Company of Edinburgh Golfers got together to draw up a list of governing rules, they felt the necessity to come up with only a handful of regulations. In the nineteenth century, control of the game passed to the Royal & Ancient Golf Club of St Andrews, whose rules are now considered the backbone of the game.

Since then, the R&A has made more than 130,000 separate adjudications as people have written in with examples of the game's list of possible variations. Few golfers, though, even tournament professionals, know all the rules. They're always falling foul of one obscure rule or another.

Know your rights

No golfer should be allowed out on to a course until he or she has a working knowledge of the rules; as much for their own benefit as anyone else's.

In every other sport, it's a case of what you can get away with by bending the rules – but not in golf. Knowing the rules is every golfer's responsibility because they are the sole arbiter of their actions. If people don't know the rules they are liable to break them, and it's a fine line between breaking rules deliberately and ignorance of them.

Here are the basic rules of golf of which you should have a working knowledge before stepping out on to the course.

KEY RULES

Rule 7: Practice

You are not allowed to practise on the course prior to playing any strokeplay competition round, nor are you permitted to walk out and test the putting surfaces of any green. If it is a 36-hole competition, no practice on the course between rounds is permitted.

Rule 8: Advice

Your opponent cannot receive advice from you to help them with their game. It's a loss-of-hole penalty in matchplay or a two-shot penalty in strokeplay competition. However, if the person who hits the shot is your partner in an event, then by all means you can ask for and receive advice. You are allowed to give factual information, though, such as the length of the hole or the position of bunkers or hazards.

Rule 10: Order of play

When standing on the first tee with your playing partners, there are a number of ways to determine who plays first. Customarily, the player with the lowest handicap will get the game under way, although you can toss a coin in the air or anything similar that appeals. Once you have all played your tee shots, the player who lies the farthest from the hole plays first, then the second farthest and so on. This continues until the hole is played out. The player who records the lowest number of strokes on that hole will play first, or

'have the honour' as it is termed, on the next tee.

If you drive the ball out-of-bounds, then you play another ball from the tee after your playing partners have driven off.

Don't worry if you accidentally play out of turn. There is no penalty, but you may be very unpopular.

Rule 11: Teeing ground

As you stand on the first tee, if you go to address your ball and knock it off its tee, you're allowed to tee it up again without penalty. If, though, you were making a swing at the ball and you knocked it 3 inches (8 cm) off the tee, it would count as one stroke.

The player with the best score at the previous hole has the honour of teeing off first at the next hole.

Rule 13: Ball played as it lies

From the moment your ball leaves the tee to when you reach the putting green, you must play it from where it lies. An exception is made during the winter months, when you will be able to improve your lie on the fairway, or follow a local rule if one is in operation. If your ball is in the trees, you must not break any branches in an effort to get a decent swing at it. The only things you are allowed to move are loose objects, such as acorns or broken twigs, but only if they don't result in your moving the ball.

When in a bunker, you are not allowed to ground the club behind the ball. You are not permitted to smooth down the sand until after you've played your shot and if your ball has landed in a footprint, then sadly that's just tough luck. You are not allowed either to move any loose impediments such as leaves, but you can move stones if there is a real danger of your striking one on your downswing.

Rules 16 and 17: Putting green

A ball on the putting green may be lifted and cleaned without penalty. A ball marker is best for this job, but anything is allowed as long as you replace the ball precisely on the spot from where you picked it up.

You can sweep away any loose impediments that lie between your ball and the hole. You may repair any pitchmarks left by inconsiderate people in front. You are not allowed to tap down any spike marks that stand on your route to the hole, however.

If you stand a long way from the hole you may either have the flag out or attended by a playing partner, who will remove it before your ball reaches the hole. If you are putting on the green and have the flag left in unattended and your ball happens to go in the hole or strikes the flagstick, then that's a two-stroke penalty. If you are having the flag out, make sure it is placed where there is no chance of your striking it with your putt; that would also be a two-stroke penalty.

When your ball is in long grass, take care that you don't inadvertantly move it when addressing the ball.

Rule 26: Water hazards

A water hazard is any sea, lake, pond, river, ditch or other open water course – whether containing water or not – and should be defined by yellow stakes. A lateral water hazard is one where it is deemed impracticable to drop the ball behind the said hazard, and should be defined by red stakes.

If your ball goes into a water hazard, you drop another ball under penalty of one stroke behind the hazard at the point of entry. What if you're not sure it went into the hazard? The rules say there must be reasonable evidence, or else you have to treat it as a lost ball. If you lose a ball, you have to go back and replay the shot from the original spot under penalty of one stroke. If your ball is lost in a lateral water hazard you must play another under penalty of one stroke within two club lengths of the point where the ball entered the hazard. If this is not possible, you can replay your shot from the original position, again adding a one-shot penalty.

Rule 27: Ball lost or out-of-bounds

You're allowed to search for five minutes for a ball. If you can't find it within that time, you have to declare it lost and play another ball from where you hit the lost one, with a one stroke penalty. If you drive from the tee into a jungle and there's little chance of finding it, you can to play a provisional ball.

You can play as many shots with this ball up to the area you lost your original. If you continue to play the provisional passed this point the original ball is declared 'lost'.

A ball is out-of-bounds if it lies wholly beyond any boundary fence or other area usually determined by white stakes. Under penalty of one stroke, you play another from the original spot.

Rule 28: Ball unplayable

You may declare your ball unplayable at any point on the course except when it is in or touching a water hazard. At this point you have three options. Under penalty of one stroke you may:

Players must be able to identify their golf ball at any given time on the golf course, particularly if it lands in a hazard.

- drop the ball within two club lengths of where the ball lies, though not nearer the hole;

- drop the ball behind the point where it lay, though keeping the trouble between yourself and the hole with no limit on how far back you can go; or

- trudge back to the spot from where you put yourself in such a mess and replay the shot.

Rule 29: Local rules

The committee of a golf club is permitted to make and publish local rules for abnormal conditions. These may be temporary measures such as allowing the lifting and cleaning of the ball in muddy conditions or to protect wildlife in environmentally sensitive areas. These are normally displayed on a board in or near the clubhouse. Other local rules may be permanent and are normally printed on the scorecard. These may include internal out-of-bounds for safety reasons or the procedure for replaying a ball that hits an overhead power cable. Read the local rules before you get to the first tee!

You should know how to drop the ball correctly when taking relief or incurring a penalty; you also need to know where to drop it.

ESSENTIAL ETIQUETTE

The etiquette of golf, its protocol, is one of the essential things that every beginner should know before setting out on his or her first round. As you learn the rules of this game, some of the ways and means will appear illogical and some unnecessary, but etiquette is not among them. At the very least, it will save you hassle from just about every other player you meet.

Shouting 'fore'

'Fore' is not a polite variation on another four-letter word, but the shout that golfers use to indicate that a ball is heading in the direction of another player, usually unsuspecting and usually on another fairway. You should never play a shot when there is a chance of hitting the players in front, but on courses where fairways are adjacent to one another, you'll occasionally – or perhaps frequently at first! – strike a shot sufficiently off-line that it may disturb the players who are on another hole, in which case you shout 'fore' as loud as you can. Etiquette such as this concerns the courtesies that one golfer has to show to another to make the game enjoyable.

Divots and pitchmarks

You'll know just how imperative etiquette should be from the moment that your first perfectly struck drive – whether it flies 300 yards (274 metres) or not – finishes in a divot that has been carelessly left by another golfer who has failed to replace the turf they sliced out of the ground when playing their shot. For a golfer, the only thing worse, perhaps, is to wander up to a greenside bunker, mentally prepared to play the shot, only to find the ball in someone else's footprint. Similarly, a green full of pitchmarks is the saddest sight.

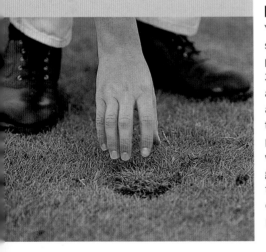

Always replace a divot carefully if you take some turf when hitting a shot. Repairing divots and pitchmarks looks after the course.

Basic courtesy

Not speaking when your playing partner is in the process of hitting a shot is an essential part of golf, as is not shuffling about on the tee when someone is about to play. The most common breach of etiquette, though, is players taking too long to play the game.

Don't let your shadow fall across the line of your partner's putt. Don't step on their line of putt. Don't throw your club in disgust after a bad shot. Stand still when players on an adjacent fairway or green are playing a shot.

ETIQUETTE – DOS

Arrive on the first tee in plenty of time for their match

Wish their playing partners good luck at the start of the round

Look out for their playing partner's golf ball

Shout 'fore' if their ball is in danger of hitting anyone

Replace divots (except on the tee)

Repair pitchmarks on the green

Leave their bag or trolley as close as possible to the next tee, but not on the green

Call the group behind through if looking for a ball

Take care not to damage the course with practice swings

AND DON'TS

Play a shot while others in front are still in range

Talk while someone is preparing to play a shot

Stand directly behind someone when they're putting

Shout or swear on the golf course

Throw clubs or equipment in temper

Replace divots on the tee

Mark their own card on the green

Laugh at another player's misfortune

Make practice swings without making sure they have room

Walk across someone's putting line on the green

Where to stand

On the tee, always stand opposite the player who is about to drive off. When you're playing your shot, make sure your partners are opposite you, too. If they're behind you, or at right angles to you, there is, at worst, the danger that you may hit them with your club on the backswing, or at best it can implant the notion in your head that you may hit them, which is the last thing you either should or want to be thinking about.

Always rake a bunker once you have played your shot so that the next person who finds the sand will have a decent lie.

Consideration of other players

Always make sure the group in front are out of range. A very rough rule of thumb here is to play when they've completed their second shots and have started walking. But in any case you'll quickly grasp how far you can hit the ball, so don't play until they've gone beyond what would be the bounds of your best drive.

When taking a practice swing, it's as well not to take huge divots out of the tees unless you desire your name to appear on a 'Wanted' poster in the head green-keeper's hut. When in the trees or in a rough area of ground, always clear twigs, pebbles, acorns or whatever you may hit either on your backswing or follow-through. These can be very dangerous both to yourself or someone else. The rules of golf do not allow you to move anything, however, that is still attached to its moorings, so don't get the machete out and start clearing branches that stand in your way or restrict your swing in any way.

On any half-decent golf course, you'll notice a rake next to every bunker. Some golfers seem to think this is merely decoration but it is, of course, to smooth over any footprints, birdprints, dogprints and holes left trying to get the ball out.

On and around the green

Repairing a pitchmark is easy. If your ball has landed on the green from a distance away then it will almost certainly have left one. Pitchmark repairers are available from any professional's shop for a nominal sum and are simple to use.

Never, under any circumstances, pull your trolley over any part of the green or leave your bag on it while you putt. Whether carrying your own clubs or using a trolley, always leave them away from the edges of the green. In the winter, you may not be able to pull a trolley if a course is wet, but if you are allowed to, don't drag it through any water or within 10 yards (10 metres) of any green.

When on the green, take care not to scrape the spikes of your shoes across the putting surface. On well-kept greens this can leave an ugly scar so do your bit by treading carefully around the hole and generally not stomping around like an elephant. Leaning on your putter while on the green or when picking the ball out of the hole are also habits that are easy to lapse into but ones to avoid.

If one of your playing partners is putting from a long distance, you could be asked to attend the flag. This involves holding it until the putt is on its way but then removing it before it reaches the hole. The edges of the holes are easy to deface, so take care that you don't damage the hole in the process of removal. As the putter has only got an area 4¼ inches (10.75 cm) wide to aim at, the last thing he or she wants is for that small target to be tampered with. Take care not to damage the edge of the hole when putting the flag back, especially in windy conditions.

Leaving your golf bag on the green is the height of bad golfing etiquette.

SLOW PLAY: THE CURSE

One thing you will quickly learn in golf is that no golfer ever admits to being a slow player. Calling a golfer slow is tantamount to questioning their parentage. When Seve Ballesteros was once told at a Tour event that he was being timed for slow play, he went bananas, threatening to play in the USA rather than Europe.

It is your duty as a considerate golfer not to cause undue delays to groups following. You can speed up your play by making shot decisions while your partner is teeing off.

Tips for sensible speed

Here are some basic tips to avoid slow play, which has become a curse in the modern game:

- if you're first or second to tee off, you should be ready – with club replaced in the bag, and bag over your shoulder or hand on trolley – to march off the moment your fourth player has completed his or her shot. This may sound a little unsociable to the last player, but it isn't. Remember: you've got at least three hours to talk to them on the golf course, never mind how much time you spend afterwards in the clubhouse;

- if you're first to tee off, don't delay everyone by marking your score for the previous hole. Do that while someone else is teeing off. When playing your second shot, don't wait until your partner has played before sizing up the wind conditions, how far you've got to go and what club to play. These are all things that can readily be done while they are playing. Be ready to hit your shot at the appropriate moment;

- on the greens, there is no need to wait for your partner to have finished their putt before reading the line of your own. Of course, there are occasions when you are on the same line, and so you cannot without committing a gross breach of etiquette, but most times you'll find you can read the green (see pages

102–105), without interrupting the thought processes of your colleague;

- if all this sounds as though you're in a race, you'll discover that on the course it's a different matter. Golf, by its very nature, is a slow and time-consuming pursuit. What's causing many of the problems is the people who abuse this basic fact, and it only takes a few golfers of this persuasion to clog up a course and so stretch out a round to five hours, and sometimes even beyond, for everyone. Few people can concentrate for that length of time and the most enjoyable rounds of golf that you experience will be the ones that take an hour less than that;

- if you're playing with two or three other players, you should wave through any group of two players, or two-ball to give it the golfing term, who are playing behind. Thus you will help to keep the traffic moving. Additionally, if your group falls one clear hole behind the players in front, be it through looking for a lost ball or simply because you are less proficient at the game, then the match behind should be invited to pass.

Start to read the line of your putt while your partner plays their shot.

SCORING

Each hole on a course has a par, or the amount of shots that it should be completed in by a professional or an amateur golfer who possesses a handicap of scratch (zero). If the par on each hole adds up to 72 after 18 holes, then it follows that the player with a handicap of scratch has to shoot 72 to live up to his or her status. Few players get to be that good.

In the beginning, you will be more than happy to average two shots above par for each hole. If you average that over three rounds that have been verified by a marker, you would be entitled to a handicap of 36 shots. As you become more proficient, your handicap will obviously come down, one day, perhaps down to a single figure – a prized possession, indeed.

Bogeys, eagles and albatrosses

To the outsider it must often seem that golf has a language all of its own and consequently a conversation between two players in a bar must be bewildering. For example: 'You were putting for an eagle on that hole, but you settled for a birdie. I once saw a man walk off with an albatross there, but I only got a par. Most times I settle for a bogey.'

As early as the 1880s, a standard score in strokes was being assigned to holes on some courses in England. In 1890, in exasperation at the level of difficulty, Major Charles Wellman, playing at Great Yarmouth, is said to have exclaimed that the standard score of the course was a regular bogey man, referring to the music-hall song 'Hush, hush, here comes the bogey man', which was popular at the time. Bogey then became the score that a good amateur should complete for the course. This was always slightly more lenient than par, which became the standard for professionals. At many courses they were one and the same thing, but not always, and for some professionals scoring bogey became second-best, a recognition that they had failed to achieve par.

Over time, then, par became accepted as the score that a good player should achieve, not just over the course of a round but on each hole. If they slipped by one stroke at that hole they had a bogey. Dropping two shots made it become a double bogey. If a player achieves one under par at a hole it is a birdie. This term dates back to 1899 and originates from the American slang word 'bird', which referred to anything wonderful. An eagle is two under par, an albatross three under.

A TYPICAL SCORECARD

❶ DISTANCE This column indicates the length of each hole in yards (metres).

❷ TEES Most golf clubs have a variety of tees to play from. Generally, the red tees are for ladies, yellow for men and white are for club competitions.

❸ STROKE INDEX This column shows you how difficult each hole is, with '1' being the most difficult and '18' the easiest.

❹ YOUR SCORE Keep a record of your own score in this column.

❺ PARTNER'S SCORE Mark your partner's score here.

❻ NET SCORE Your net score is your actual score minus your handicap.

❼ SIGNATURE You should always check your score very carefully before signing a scorecard. Although in competitions, someone else will be marking your card, it is your responsibility to make sure that the information recorded is correct. Once you have put your signature on the bottom of the card, the score stands.

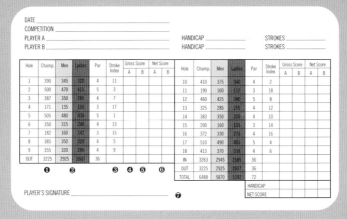

DATE _____
COMPETITION _____
PLAYER A _____ HANDICAP _____ STROKES _____
PLAYER B _____ HANDICAP _____ STROKES _____

Hole	Champ.	Men	Ladies	Par	Stroke Index	Gross Score A	Gross Score B	Net Score A	Net Score B	Hole	Champ.	Men	Ladies	Par	Stroke Index	Gross Score A	Gross Score B	Net Score A	Net Score B
1	390	345	320	4	11					10	410	375	340	4	2				
2	500	470	415	5	3					11	190	160	112	3	18				
3	387	350	285	4	7					12	460	425	380	5	8				
4	171	135	110	3	17					13	325	285	255	4	12				
5	505	480	435	5	1					14	383	350	300	4	10				
6	350	315	290	4	13					15	200	160	125	3	14				
7	182	160	142	3	15					16	372	330	270	4	16				
8	385	350	320	4	5					17	510	490	465	5	4				
9	355	320	290	4	9					18	413	370	338	4	6				
OUT	3225	2925	2607	36						IN	3263	2945	2585	36					
	❶	❷		❸ ❹ ❺		❻				OUT	3225	2925	2607	36					
										TOTAL	6488	5870	5192	72					
										HANDICAP									
										NET SCORE									

PLAYER'S SIGNATURE _____ ❼

COURSE MANAGEMENT

Being able to plot your way around a golf course from the first hole to the 18th green, safely avoiding the pitfalls of bunkers, rough, lakes and ditches, requires patience, planning and intelligence.

Collectively, this is called good course management and it's something at which every top player excels. Good golf is smart golf, and to become a really good player you must learn a wide range of course-management skills.

Work your way back from green to tee

When standing on the tee, players should have a strategy or game-plan for every hole:

- decide which side of the fairway offers the best angle of attack into the green. For example, if there are bunkers protecting the front right side of the green, it will obviously be safer to hit an approach shot from the left side of the fairway, where it won't be necessary to carry the ball over the sand;

- make sure that there are no hazards, such as fairway bunkers or lakes, waiting to catch you. If the chosen route does encounter hazards, you can either select a club that won't reach the hazards, or play well away from the trouble. If the hazards are too great, you may want to rethink your shot strategy. The best players are those who have a game-plan but who aren't afraid to change it if necessary.

PLOT YOUR COURSE

If you watch golf tournaments on television, you will notice that the pros don't always aim at the flag when they're hitting their approach shots into the greens. The reason for this is because the greenkeepers like to place the pin in a really difficult position on the green – for example, just behind a bunker or right next to the water. These are called 'sucker pins' because only a sucker would aim at them.

You will also notice that on sloping greens the pros always try to leave their approach shots on the low side of the hole. An uphill putt is generally easier to control than a downhill one.

The considerable variety that exists in all 18 holes makes it necessary to think your way around a course.

Smart play

In such situations, the professionals normally aim at the safe part of the green because they know that, if they aim at the flag and mis-hit their shot, they will probably end up in the sand or the water. This is not negative play – it's smart play.

Make the worst score a bogey

On running into trouble on the golf course, many golfers make things worse by trying to play a miraculous recovery shot. Colin Montgomerie's attitude to a poorly played shot is instructive: he will make sure that his worst score on the hole is a bogey. For example, if Monty hits his tee shot into the trees on a par four (which he doesn't do very often) and has no safe route to the green, he will play a shot that enables him to go for the green with his third shot – even if it means chipping out sideways to get back on to the fairway.

This does not mean that you should settle for making a bogey every time you hit a wayward shot. On the contrary. Much of the fun in golf comes from using the imagination to conjure up adventurous recovery shots. However, you should carefully weigh up your chances of pulling off the shot. If in doubt, take the safe option and make the worst score a bogey.

Allow for a 'flyer' out of long grass
Many players do not expect to be able to hit the ball very far out of long grass, but occasionally the exact opposite happens and the ball flies farther than from a clean lie on the fairway. This is known as a 'flyer', and it happens when blades of grass get trapped between the ball and the clubface at impact. This situation prevents the grooves from imparting backspin on the ball. As a result, the ball travels farther than normal. Longer grass can grasp the clubhead, closing it as the shot is played and dragging the ball to the left. Open the clubface a little and aim slightly right.

Laying up on long par fives
A good habit is laying up to your favourite distance on par fives. If the green is well out of reach, this tactic can be a very positive move. Rather than trying to blast the ball as far up the fairway as possible and bringing all kinds of hazards into play, most top players will deliberately try to leave themselves a full shot of around 100 yards (91 metres) into the green. So if the green is out of reach, play a shot that will then enable you to play an approach shot into the green with your favourite club.

Take full advantage of the teeing area
In golf, every detail counts. Depending on the shape of the hole, most top players will tee up on the side of the teeing area that gives them the safest route to the fairway.

Tom Lehman, for example, likes to draw the ball – curve it from right to left in the air – so he will usually set up on the left side of the teeing area, and aim down the right edge of the fairway. This way he has the whole fairway at which to aim. Remember that the ball must be teed up between the two markers or up to two club-lengths behind, but the player's feet may be outside the markers. You will occasionally see professionals doing this to maximize their strategic use of the tee.

GLOSSARY

Albatross A score of three under par on a hole.

Approach shot A shot from close to the green that should, if played well, land on the putting surface.

Back nine The second set of nine holes on an 18-hole golf course.

Birdie A score of one under par on a hole.

Bogey A score of one over par on a hole.

Borrow The amount a putt will deviate due to the slope of the green.

Carry The distance from when a ball is struck to when it first lands.

Chip A low-running shot played from around the green to the putting surface.

Dog-leg A hole that changes direction, either to the left or the right, halfway through its course.

Double bogey A score of two over par on a hole.

Draw A specialist shot in which the ball curves from right to left in the air.

Eagle A score of two under par on a hole.

Fade A specialist shot in which the ball curves from left to right in the air.

Fairway The area of mown turf between tee and green.

Fourball A match between two teams of two players, each playing their own ball.

Foursome A match between two teams of two players, each playing one ball by alternate shots.

Fringe The area of fairly short grass between the green and the fairway.

Front nine The opening nine holes on an 18-hole golf course.

Green An area of closely mown grass prepared for putting.

Handicap The scoring system whereby players can take on each other and the course on level terms. The worse a player is, the higher the handicap and the more shots he or she receives. If someone regularly goes around a course in 20 shots over par, then they should have a handicap of 20 and will receive 20 shots towards their efforts of matching the par of the course.

Hook A mistimed shot that deviates severely to the left for a right-handed player.

Lie The situation in which a ball finishes after the playing of a stroke.

Long iron A description for those irons numbered one to four.

Mid-iron A description for those irons numbered five to seven.

Out-of-bounds The area of the course outside the boundary lines. It is normally indicated by a series of white stakes.

Par The standard score for each hole, and the entire course.

Pitch A lofted shot from around the green to the putting surface.

Pitchmark The indentation caused when the ball lands on the green after an approach shot.

R&A The game's governing body, the Royal & Ancient Golf Club of St Andrews.

Rough The area of unmown grass that lies either side of the fairway.

Shank A totally mistimed shot, usually made with a short iron, in which the ball comes off the junction between hosel and clubface and travels at right angles to the target intended.

Short iron A description for those irons numbered eight and nine as well as the pitching wedge, sand wedge and any other wedges.

Slice A mistimed shot in which the ball deviates sharply to the right for a right-handed player.

Strokeplay The form of the game in which the number of strokes played is the determining factor.

Sweet spot The optimum spot in the middle of the clubhead where the greatest possible mass can be delivered from the clubface to the ball.

Tee The closely mown area where the first stroke on a hole is played. The ball is generally played from a tee peg.

USGA United States Golf Association, the game's governing body in North America.

INDEX

PICTURE ACKNOWLEDGEMENTS

Main Photography © Octopus Publishing Group Limited/ Mark Newcombe

Other Photography by:
Octopus Publishing Group Limited/Angus Murray 1–125/ Nick Walker 36 left, 36 right, 37 bottom right, 37 bottom left, 37 bottom centre, 56 bottom left, 57 left, 57 right, 57 centre, 59 bottom right, 59 bottom left, 59 bottom centre, 60 top, 60 bottom, 63 top left, 63 top right, 63 bottom right, 63 bottom left, 70 bottom right, 71 bottom right, 71 bottom left, 72 bottom left, 73 left, 73 right, 99 bottom right, 99 bottom left, 100, 101 left, 101 right, 102, 116, 117,99 top.
Visions In Golf Picture Library/ Mark Newcombe 27 top left, 27 top right, 27 bottom right, 27 bottom left, 28 top left, 28 top right, 28 bottom right, 28 bottom left, 29 top, 29 bottom.

PUBLISHER'S ACKNOWLEDGEMENTS

Executive editor Trevor Davies
Project editor Alice Bowden
Design manager Tokiko Morishima
Designer Ben Cracknell
Picture library manager Jennifer Veall
Production manager Ian Paton